BECOME A SUCCESSFUL INDIE AUTHOR

CRAIG MARTELLE

"Da, would you have listened to me? I think not. I tried several times to broach the subject, but you just shooed me away. You aren't that easy to talk with, Da. I know you have much on your mind, so I don't fault you, but it would be nice to have someone I could talk to. I have always had Ian and Alana, but now that they are gone. I feel all alone in the world."

Fergus looked at his daughter with new eyes. He had always just taken for granted that she would do as she was told. He never thought about her feelings or desires. It was not the way of the world for children to be included in decision making for their own futures. Maybe that was wrong, he thought. Maybe, we should be asking their opinions instead of just doing what we feel is right. Now his friend had lost his youngest son. True, he had other sons to inherit his property and title and take over his laird's responsibilities, but he had still lost his youngest. Fergus believed that Ian had been Angus' favorite son as well. He was certainly taking the news hard.

Chapter 2

The days passed, as they are wont to do. Diana continued her duties as chatelaine of her father's keep. Her father continued his duties as laird. They rarely saw Angus MacAllister. Fergus heard that Angus was drinking a lot and had become surly and hard to deal with. He was sad to hear that his old friend was in that condition, but there was little he could do.

Several months later in August, Diana received a letter from Ian all the way from America, a place called Virginia.

> *Dearest Diana,*
>
> *I am writing to let you know how grateful Alana and I are to you for giving us this wonderful opportunity. We were married in Inverness two days after leaving you.*

Copyright © 2018 Craig Martelle
All rights reserved.

Editing services provided by Mia Darien – miadarien.com
Cover by Sapphire Designs
Formatting by Drew Avera Formatting - facebook.com/drewaveraformatting
Illustrations done in Canva.

This is a book on writing books. If that wasn't your desire in buying this eBook, then please return it within seven days for a full refund from Amazon.

OVERVIEW

1. Writing your book – aka, telling the story

- Great first line, first paragraph, first page
- Testing a Minimum Viable Product
- Preparing to Write
- Writing the Story
- Getting Feedback
- Discipline
- Finish It
- Detail tracking (story dictionary)

2. Creating your Brand (your persona)

- What is your brand?
- Building Your Email List
- Newsletter
- Other ways to have people follow you
- Selling Books at a Convention
- Pen Name

3. The business-side of being an author

- Defining Success
- Where does the data come from?
- Expenses and Revenue
- Organizing your business so you have a place to put that revenue and deduct those expenses
- Tracking Data
- Organizing your business is about managing risk
- SWOT Analysis of Your Business
- Sphere of Control - Sphere of Influence
- Representative Business Structure by Joe Solari
- Managing Your Taxes
- Taxes
- Copyright & Keeping Your Books Safe

4. Publishing on Amazon

- Launch Checklist
- Cover Art
- Title
- Keywords
- Blurb
- Categories
- Age & Grade
- Digital Rights Management
- Upload your eBook
- Other Upload Issues
- Launch Pricing
- Resources for going wide (on all platforms, versus Amazon exclusive)
- Release Schedule
- Serials and an 18-Day Release Schedule

5. Building a following

- Biggest Bang for the Buck
- Snippets, Blogs, and Social Media – Oh my!
- How do you build a following?
- Newsletter Cross Promotion
- New Release Notification
- Getting Feedback
- Trolls

6. Writing the next book

- Keeping Your Goals Alive
- Writing a new story (the power of a backlist)
- Improving Your Word Count
- Social Proof
- Staying Motivated (without Alienating your family)
- Hitting the Wall
- The Value of Time

7. Marketing

- Return on Investment
- Margin
- Amazon Ads
- Facebook Ads
- BookBub Ads

8. Random Stuff, Other Words and Definitions

- Author Rank
- Collaborating
- Bestseller Lists
- Conventions & Professional Organizations

- Random Rants

Bibliography
Appendix A – Acronyms Used in this Book
Appendix B – Synonyms for Said, Yell, & Move
Appendix C – Notes on Conference Planning
Author Notes

FOREWORD BY MICHAEL ANDERLE

A long time ago, I was a computer programmer. In the late 90's there were a set of books (I want) to say were called "1001 Tips for ...".

I loved these books! Why? Because they were laid out in such a way that I could quickly find out if my questions were answered inside the books themselves. Mind you, this was before the internet when you could just Google an answer.

The books, unfortunately, didn't make it much longer once the Internet became common place and I really regret that.

Not that I regret not having a huge book of paper, but rather I regret losing them because the layout was so important to my early work success and I can point to those books, those questions, and the answers.

Did I have a printing problem? Go to chapter 10 on Printing. A GUI question? That was chapter 3 and so on.

It didn't matter that ten minutes before, I didn't know how to handle the printing problem. What mattered was I knew how to find out the answer and how to get the answer fast.

All of the information inside of the book can be found 'out there' somewhere. However, it is Craig's experience in bringing together the right information, organized in the right way, with personal clarity and examples from his experience that makes this book worth picking up.

Whether you are a new Indie Publisher or have published a few books, there is good information inside these pages.

Items we all forget, from time to time.

Mistakes made you will want to skip, so learn from those of us who have made them in the first place.

I've been blessed to have benefited from Craig's business acumen (which he spent decades learning) inside my company LMBPN Publishing for free.

(Because I can be a cheap bastard like that. All I owe him is a beer, and since we see each other so infrequently, he rarely remembers and even if he does, a few beers is WAY cheaper than his consulting rate so I come out ahead anyway.)

Take a few minutes to review the questions he answers in the front of this book. See if any of them look like a question you already have, or believe you might want to know. If you, like me, appreciate someone collating the knowledge and save you time and energy looking it up then next time you see him, buy him a beer for me, would you?

It will take another beer off the tab I owe him.

Ad Aeternitatem,
  Michael Anderle

FOREWORD BY KEVIN MCLAUGHLIN

Step 1: Imagine a Venn diagram, with two circles. One circle is the things that people like to read. The other circle is the things you like to write. Where they overlap? Write that.

Step 2: When picking your genre, be prepared to write at LEAST six books in that specific sub-genre before moving on. If you move on that early, move to a closely related genre. For example, writing six space opera books and moving to military SF is fine. Moving from SO to epic fantasy is likely going to damage your brand and slow your growth. There are tons of exceptions to this, authors who have crossed genres and killed it anyway. They did that *in spite of* the cross-genre work. You maximize your success by building a brand

within a single type of book. Expand later, after you have a dozen or more books out.

Step 3: Write a great story that people want to read. To do this, you need a deep understanding of plot structure—or you need to get very lucky. Study structure and form. Understand the Hero's Journey. Read McKee and "Save the Cat" and Libbie Hawker and every other major type of plotting and structure tool. Study them, especially the renowned ones that have stood the test of time. YES, even if you are a "pantser." In fact, it's even MORE crucial that pantsers grok plot and structure, since they're flying by the seat of their pants and need an intuitive understanding of those things.

Step 4: Get a great, GENRE-SPECIFIC cover for the book. The primary thing every cover must do is tell any prospective reader precisely what sort of book this is. Ideally, it should look a lot like bestselling books in your sub-sub-sub-genre. You want a cover that tells the readers immediately what they are getting, with no questions or doubts.

Step 5: Publish. Then market. Your job as publisher is to first put out a top quality product: well-edited, however you make that happen, with a great cover and good blurb. Then it's to get eyes on that product. That's all the book is, once you upload it. It is a product that you must show to potential consumers to get them to buy it. Facebook ads, AMS ads, Twitter ads, Adsense, and anything else you can think of. Drive readers to that book page in enough numbers, with good enough targeting, and you will move copies.

Step 6: While you're marketing, be writing. Same genre. Same series. Get more books out. What I am seeing today is four books a year is the bare minimum to have a decent shot at financial/career success. Less than that and you're losing momentum too fast. The good news? Four books at 75k words each is only about 800 words per day. You can pound that out on lunch breaks, if you want this badly enough. If you don't want it badly enough, you won't do the work and it won't happen.

The question will usually come down to this one: how hungry are you?

The people who work the hardest are generally the ones who are succeeding the most. They're not always the best writers. Nor are they always the best marketers or publishers. But over time, the simple application of effort has a multiplicative impact on one's march toward success.

More insight here from Hugh Howey - http://www.hughhowey.com/writing-insights-part-one-becoming-a-writer/

INTRODUCTION

Who am I to give advice on being a successful independently-published author (indie)? I have more than two million words in publication. Here are the covers of some of my books. I write every day. I publish. I market. I run my business, and I make good money at it. Hopefully, this book will put some of your fears to rest and get you on track toward the next level as a professional author.

Why publish your books yourself? For the same reason most small businesses start—you have an idea and are the best one to make it a reality. That idea is a story, and you have to write it, then publish it, and then sell it. And then write another one.

Daunting? Maybe.

Easy? Definitely not.

Doable? Eminently.

We publish independently because we get a much higher royalty share, we have complete control over our work, we interact directly with our readership, and

INTRODUCTION

so much more. The drawback is that you have to do it all yourself—creativity, production, marketing, and accounting. But indies are betting on themselves, just like any other small business. We stand up and shout, "I got this!" Then we knuckle down and do the hard work where we and we alone are responsible for our success.

Will this book guarantee that you'll be the next seven-figure author? Absolutely not. But it will show you that if you work hard at the right things, it may not be as far away as you think. Make your hard work work for you.

This book is meant to show you what's possible, and that you're not alone on this journey. Arming yourself with information is the best way to win the battle known as "Indie Publishing."

You can do it. It takes work, but the mountain is not insurmountable.

JK Rowling made over one billion dollars ($1,000,000,000) in book sales alone and estimates suggest that she reached only nine percent of the book reading public. Only nine percent is worth a billion dollars. She didn't get there because she was trying to get rich. She got there because she wrote great stories and then handled the business side of it.

What if you were able to tap $1/10,000^{th}$ of what JK Rowling tapped?

Then you would be a $100,000 author. The average author makes less than $10,000 a year. But we refuse to be average, because we learn from others with readily available information that will help us get to that next level.

No matter where you are on your author journey, there's always a new level you can reach.

Is this a how-to book? Kind of. As an indie, don't trust anyone who speaks in absolutes. There are a lot of things that you should do, and inside this book, I'll highlight those very clearly. This book is more like a smorgasbord—pick and choose what may work best for you. Tweak as you need and take it for a test drive. Remember—one size *does not* fit all.

INTRODUCTION

The more you know about your business, the more time you can devote to what brought you here in the first place—your writing. I love to write. It's my escape from everything else, but I also love the business side of things.

You'll find that no early mistake can't be overcome through adjustment and reengagement. Your first book doesn't sell well. So what? Learn why, fix it, and get better for next time.

There are many different ways up the mountain, so do what works best for your business. I write pulp, but I take my craft seriously. Doing what keeps your readers most engaged is what you must to do to make money at your craft. You. This is your story and your business. Read as many success stories as you can, see what works for others, and build your plan on the details, not the results. Control what you can control and then do what you need to do. The results can only come from that.

Roll up your sleeves, because it's time to get to work.

ONE

WRITING YOUR BOOK – AKA, TELLING THE STORY

- Great First Line
- Testing a Minimum Viable Product
- Preparing to Write
- Writing the Story
- Getting Feedback
- Discipline
- Finish It
- Detail Tracking (story dictionary)

Great First Line

Where do we start? With the first word.

"It was the best of times. It was the worst of times." The first two sentences of Dickens's classic, *A Tale of Two Cities*.

It grips. It creates a dichotomy. You have to read on.

Everything you write is to get the reader to keep reading. From the first sentence to the next, they need to keep reading to find out what happens.

I bought a book on how to write better-converting emails. That should have been an author's best friend, but what it was was seventy pages of "can't believe that's true? Read on!" It was a complete book of clickbait. That's not what I'm talking about. Don't try to put a cliffhanger at the end of each sentence, unless you do and it works. You want them to keep turning the page.

What you want to do is create characters that readers can relate to and a storyline that flows.

Scenery, spelling, good grammar. All those take a backseat to the story. Of course you should try to produce a completely error-free book, but you should ask the question: whose definition of error? That's why they're called typos, a minor miscue that is easily remedied once you know where it is. But when you have a story that pulls the reader in, they'll keep reading, right through any typos.

Testing a Minimum Viable Product

When Michael Anderle—author of the mega-bestselling *Kurtherian Gambit* series—talks about a minimum viable product, he's talking about a story that keep readers turning the page. Getting beta readers on board early in the process is important to optimize your writing time. If three people who are mostly in your genre unanimously agree that they want to keep reading after they've seen the first three thousand (3000) words, then keep writing, and continue to write.

If they say that they wouldn't keep reading, then you have an issue that needs to be fixed. Your product may not be viable.

At that point, nothing can help you except fixing your product (your story). Rapid release, Facebook Ads, newsletter (NL) swaps—nothing will save your book. You need to write a good story, one that people want to keep reading. It can be in need of editing—that's okay, because you can get that done later before you hit publish—but rewriting a book in entirety that readers have panned is not just time-consuming, it's soul-crushing.

Getting out of the gates with your first book will almost always take longer than when you're more experienced, and it's okay. It doesn't have to be perfect, just good enough. If you're paralyzed by fear and self-doubt, write those first words and make them killer. Then share. I think you'll find that there's a storyteller inside of you. Listen to the feedback, hit some singles, doubles, and then swing for the fence.

How do you find test readers? Ask other new authors struggling with their first book, swap and read. Ask readers in your genre. For me, Facebook was great to connect with fellow fans of Andre Norton, but be aware that their standard is Andre Norton. Striking up a conversation with these folks can lead to finding a few new test readers, but be patient. Cultivate that over time by finding other authors you like, favorite stories and the like.

Look at the book from a reader's perspective. Me personally? I care what readers in my genre think first and foremost because they are the ones paying for my books. That is the one hard and fast rule—you must find readers willing to buy your books. Otherwise, it's just a hobby, which is okay. But if you want to make money at this thing called self-publishing, then you need to find people who like what they see well enough to part with some of their cash.

Minimum viable product—a story that people want to keep reading. Period.

Preparing to Write

What do you do with a three-hour block of writing time? I suggest you read something from your genre for the first hour, a bunch of different passages from your genre. Get on the mailing lists —FreeBooksy, BookBub, ReadCheaply, BargainBooksy, and others. They send a daily email. You can get frontline, top-notch authors in your genre for free or $0.99. If you don't read in your genre, how can you write in it? That's my opinion. It helps to see what others are doing, if nothing else, to see what you can do better. If you are doing a mash-up between genres, read both. First and foremost, I believe authors are readers.

I write in Microsoft Word. It's what I've used ever since it came out. CreateSpace has templates for paperbacks. I downloaded one of those after I published my first book and that's what I write in—a CS Word template for a 6" by 9" book. There are a lot of other programs out there to use, but remember that they are all tools. Do not let the tool dictate your story, let the tool help you tell it. Whether you use Libre Office, Google Docs, Scrivener, or any of the others, make sure you teach it who's the boss.

Most software programs come with free 30-day trials. Try one and see if you can produce a small sample of your book—a chapter or two with front matter and end matter—in the proper format. If you can use a tool, upload your manuscript into the website of your chosen distributor(s) (Kindle Direct Publishing, Nook, Kobo), and see the final product (.MOBI, epub), then you've mastered your tool.

Get your words down, because you can't edit a blank page. I think a page full of bad words is still a good page, because I can rewrite it and that goes more quickly than creating it from scratch. Even if I end up changing every word.

I believe you should write every single day. It's what writers do. It's an escape. If you only wrote 1000 words a day, that's 365,000 words over the course of a year. That is a lot of words. That could be from 30 minutes to an hour of jamming. Some days, I only get a couple hundred words, and that's okay. There are plenty of other days where I get a lot of words.

I used to pants it, seat of my pants, but I don't have the luxury of unlimited time anymore. When I'm in the zone, a moment of exceptional clarity, I will write an outline from start to finish. Usually it's a rambling narrative with bad grammar and ridiculously long run-on sentences, but it is a complete story. I've written up to 10,000 word outlines, which makes writing the book so much easier. I am now including the outline in my books as bonus material, because the end story will deviate some from the original idea. The reader can see what I was thinking originally and then how it turned out. I am now an outliner for the simple reason that it saves me time.

Know your story before you start writing. Grip your readers right out of the gate. I write the first chapter—usually short, with action, brief dialogue, emotional conflict, and lots of unanswered questions. I then write the last chapter of the book—I have to detail how and where I want the story to end. All the rest makes up the learning journey that I take with my readers.

Knowing the story you want to tell and knowing all the details are not the same thing.

As part of my outlines, I will include key learning points, what I want to give the readers. Here's a sample of what I wrote today for Darklanding Book 9.

Thad calls Shaunte and tells her that she makes him want to retire from being a soldier. She's humbled, but tells him that's who he is and taking that away from him would make him miserable and resent her. Just like she is a businessman first and foremost. It's in her blood like being a warrior is in his. He formally asks her out on a date. The scene ends with her in her office, thinking about it, smiling.

And that's the extent of my outline, but fleshing it out will come to when I start writing. I can see the scene because I've lived the scene. Write what you know has worked well for me. While deployed, it's nice to talk with your wife and dream about being home. While home, doing the everyday life things, it's easy to dream about being back in the war. Capturing the flashes of what people see and feel during those times will make for a nice chapter.

Writing the Story

How do you tell your story without creating discord? There are innumerable ways to create flow and even more ways to ruin the story's flow. Let me give a couple of examples here, but your genre will be more tuned in to what those readers expect.

I have a list of words that I can use instead of the word "said." But digging out synonyms isn't the right answer. What you're looking for is flow, telling a gripping story that keeps the readers engaged.

<u>Imagine a group of three people talking.</u>

"I'm hungry," the young man said.

"I'm not," his father replied.

"I wouldn't eat what I'm smelling," the young man's sister said.

<u>That prose seems stilted. Let's color it in.</u>

"I'm hungry," the young man said, sniffing the air to catch the scent coming from the kitchen.

"I'm not." His father wrinkled his nose and grimaced.

"I wouldn't eat what I'm smelling," the young man's sister retorted, taking a step backward, away from the kitchen.

<u>Or an alternative.</u>

The young man stood in the doorway, sniffing appreciatively. "I'm hungry."

"I'm not!" The young man's father wrinkled his nose and grimaced.

"I wouldn't eat what I'm smelling!" The young man's sister took a step backward, away from the kitchen.

Let me recommend the *Story Grid: What Good Editors Know* by Shawn Coyne for more information on crafting a tale. Joe Nassise and Max Drake also have a great deal to offer in the world of craft. (Look for links and such in the bibliography.) The above is only one example of an infinite number. See the difference, look to your genre, and embrace a style that you like best.

Craft is critically important, but it is also unique to your genre. Lawyers write a certain way because they have to. Urban Fantasy is different from High Fantasy is different from Hard Science Fiction is different from Romance is different from... You get the idea.

Know what expectations there are within your genre. Study your genre– NO! Study it, don't just read the books. What are the tropes?

What is the most common writing style? You need to be unique, but not too different, and that is my blue collar approach. You want fresh stories told in a great way that is still within a style that readers expect.

K-Lytics published a great report on what it took to make $100,000 per year. Their conclusion based on the considerable data available to them? Publish great books frequently. Now that is the challenge, isn't it? How can we make sure that our books get better and better?

Getting Feedback

Look for people who are able to talk about the story. Nearly every story is salvageable with the right advice.

Be open to feedback. If you have to explain, then you wrote it incorrectly, unless that's what you were going for, and then you need to find the readers who you don't have to explain it to. The story and characters must stand on their own. On rare occasions, the reader will miss something. Think how you can help future readers avoid making the same mistake.

I sold my very first story to a traditional publishing house, a small press. It has a 4.0 rating on Amazon, not too bad at all, but I look back through it and it makes me wince to read my own words. I could rewrite the whole series over the course of a week or two and smooth everything out, but that's not exactly the point. Those books are good stories in survival fiction, although one reviewer said that they made me the laughingstock of an entire state. My biggest fans from End Times Alaska are Alaskans, so I think that reviewer is one of those outliers who enjoy trying to make themselves the subject matter expert.

I'm a fiction author. Fine. My story didn't meet with your idea of how things would go. Easy day. We both move on. Life is still good.

This is one of the hardest things to do. You are going to take your baby, your story, and throw it out there for the unwashed masses to criticize. But they aren't unwashed masses. They are good people like you and me. Some may take pleasure in being negative, but you'll find there are many more people who are willing to talk about the positive.

Look at the negatives and see what they tell you. Look at the positives and see what they tell you. Somewhere in between is the truth. I have a number of books with a 4.9 star rating. I am humbled by the overwhelmingly positive response. In those cases, I talk with my editor to find what I did differently and then we try to leverage more of that in the next book.

Maintaining a constant dialogue with your editor is key to improvement. Let me share some feedback that I received today when I asked a friend to look at the start to a new story.

Your writing is astounding, Craig. You have come a very long way from your first work which was excellent in its own right. I love the third-person omniscient perspective and the colorful commentary on the town as they come to port. By the time they reach the mayor I feel like I know the characters. An interesting bit of writer's magic there.

I expect you know how this made me feel. I have worked hard over the years to improve my prose. Listening to my editors (I have multiple, but it took time and money to bring the team together), listening to the readers, reading, and practicing. Always practicing.

How does one get an editor or team of editors? On the 20Booksto50k Facebook group, I started a self-promotion thread for editors to advertise. Anyone can peruse those posts and select a number of editors to try. Nearly all of them will do a sample of five hundred or one thousand words. Find one that seems to suit you best, as in the one who helps bring out the best version of you as a writer.

I've found more. I have developmental editors who help me keep my story on track. They do that for free because they like my stuff, and I like them. I don't want to ever let the Double Ds down by telling a bad or confusing story. The Darklanding series is for them. It was their idea and I wanted to see them smile, so we made it come to life. When your editors become your close friends, everyone gets better.

For a single-pass line editor, you get a certain amount of proofing and grammar correction. For a double-pass, you'll get continuity and even better spelling and grammar alignment. It'll cost you more, so you have to assess if you received that much more value for your money. I'm good with a single-pass and a good group of beta readers.

Keep searching until you find an editor who you can work with. Talk about your schedule and don't ever deliver a manuscript late or in sub-standard condition. Treat your editor with respect and you'll be amazed at how great they can help you become.

Discipline

Being an indie means being all things. It means writing most of all. Telling the stories that become the product that bring in revenue to help you keep writing. Too many people never finish their book or finish it only to throw it aside because it's not a masterpiece.

Expect that some of the words will be horrible, and that's okay. We've all written words that make us do a double-take. What in the hell was I thinking? Find the good in the words. Find the smooth plot. If it's not there, fix it. You have the power. If you have a half-done book, finish it.

Don't be the writer who can't finish a story. You had a great idea once. Embrace it and bring it to fruition. Flesh out your characters. Bring them to life. Writing is how we escape. Reading is how our fans escape.

It's hard work, but once you're done, you'll find that you've accomplished something that almost no one else has. Look at the rest of the world. Seven billion people and Amazon shows titles from millions of authors. If you finish a book and publish it, that makes you one in a thousand. That means you are different from 99.9% of the people out there, many who said they wanted to write a book. If you make enough to write full-time, that makes you one in a million. But you can't get there if you don't finish books.

Be a published author. It's the first plateau on the mountain of success. Join us, but it takes finishing the book before anything else. It takes writing, even when sometimes you don't feel like it. For me, that's when my most profound words seem to appear. On my editing pass, I can see what mood I was in when I wrote the scenes.

The readers can't tell because they take the book as a single escape from their world. How do I know that? Because I published, people read my stories, and I hear from them, both good and bad. It all makes me better, and it started with writing that first book, from start to finish.

Finish It

If you start a story and it isn't doing what you want it to do, you have three choices: rewrite it, keep going to the finish, or abandon it.

Rewriting a story when you're in the middle guarantees that it will be a long and painful book. It's also the perfectionist's nightmare—a book that will never measure up.

If you've written to the minimum viable product level, then someone has already told you that they'd like to read on. What was sufficiently gripping to keep them interested? Do more of that. I know that sounds simplistic, but it could be that easy.

Readers have their expectations that start with the genre they think the book is in and with the framework you establish in the first chapter. Don't try to build the entire world with a massive info dump in the first few pages. I would never recommend that—which is how I look at it as a reader.

Let me go to the first book in The Bad Company series. Here's what I have for the first page and a half. I introduce three characters and a situation. The rest of the book resolves what you see in the introduction.

1. Combat action
2. A mission determined by someone not in the battle
3. Humor – "not that one, the other one..."

Everything that will make up the book is there—Terry, Nathan, Lance, combat, and humor. It is a military science fiction book, heavy on the military, but it's also space opera, hence the introduction of the characters, even though most of the readership already knows who they are. We wanted to bring in new readers, so made this an entry point into the series without having to read the previous thirteen books.

But those are marketing issues and what we want to talk about is finishing the book. When the readers looked at the first couple pages below, they see the hook of the story, the issues that need to be resolved. As long as the story was working toward that end, then it was going to remain a sound story.

An explosion sounded and plasma fire flashed before his eyes.

Hidden in a remote corner of the Pan Galaxy, Nathan Lowell sat in his private office looking at the video communication screen. The President of the Bad Company frowned.

His Direct Action Branch was engaged and not in a good way. Nathan slowly shook his head as he watched.

Thirty-seven star systems away, General Lance Reynolds saw the same images displayed on his monitor. He chewed vigorously on his cigar. The report wasn't what he had expected.

Colonel Terry Henry Walton, the man in the image, looked back and forth between the screen and something to his left. Ominous sounds accompanied the image.

"This first mission wasn't what we contracted for, Nathan," Terry yelled at the portable console that sat with a sideways tilt. He stared at a point off-screen, shook his head, and continued. "My first stop when I get off this rock is that dandy president's office where I'll wring his pencil-neck to get our thirty percent bonus and seventy percent kicker. And then I'm leveling his fucking palace!"

"Can you settle this with what you have?" Lance asked.

"Yes, sir," Terry replied.

"I already told you once, call me Lance."

"No can do, General. Can't have you thinking I've grown soft just because I've been a pseudo-civilian for over a hundred and fifty years. Hang on." Terry's smile evaporated as he looked off-screen, his lip curling involuntarily. "SHOOT HIM!" he shouted.

The crack of hand-held railguns answered. Terry stabbed his finger at something neither Nathan nor Lance could see.

"Not that one, the other one," Terry corrected. More cracks from the hypervelocity weapons. Terry nodded and flipped the bird. "Fuck you, buddy, and your stupid-looking stalk-head!"

Terry turned back to the screen. "Where were we?"

I wrote that first and then edited it often in order to help create the smoothest flow possible. And then I wrote the last chapter, which you see below.

1. So much combat that they were exhausted from fighting
2. Mission accomplished
3. They still have some humor

Terry's head hung as he sat at the conference table. Micky didn't know if he was awake or not. Char sat up straight, but her eyes were closed and her mouth hung slack as she was out cold.

The captain watched them briefly, believing that they hadn't slept for the entire time they'd been on the planet.

"Smedley, activate the comm system and link us through, please."

Nathan appeared and gave Captain Micky San Marino a hearty good morning. Micky smiled and pointed the camera at the leaders of the Bad Company's Direct Action Branch. Nathan watched them, shaking his head.

Micky got up and walked behind the two, putting his hands gently on their shoulders. Terry about came out of his skin, making the captain jump back, stumble, and slam into the wall.

Terry mumbled an apology before blinking the hologram into focus. "Oh! Hi, Nathan. How's it hanging?"

"You've looked better, TH. Although Char is spectacular as always. I don't know why she strapped herself to a goon like you."

The whites of Char's eyes showed round as she forced her eyes open, making her look like a zombie.

Which was exactly how she felt.

Terry turned his head, saw her vacant expression, and started to chuckle.

"You have a way with words," Terry started, before taking a deep breath and repeating the report that he'd prepared in his head.

After two minutes, Nathan stopped him.

"You know who Ronald Reagan was. Remember when he asked for the entire budget of the United States to be condensed down to one page? Give me that version."

"We ended the war and we made more than we spent. We acquired a Podder and a Crooner for the team. They bring unique capabilities, diversity, strength of mind and character, all of that. I don't think we'll be misled again into fighting some knucklehead's war for him. Were you able to talk with dickface?"

"You mean the president?" Nathan asked, knowing exactly what Terry Henry meant.

The colonel nodded. Nathan leaned close to his monitor. Char hadn't blinked. He was convinced that she was sound asleep with her eyes wide open. He looked back to Terry.

"Yes. He's pleased with the outcome and delivered an abject apology. He said that he wasn't deliberately misleading. I don't believe him, but we have our money in hand including the bonus and kicker. Your first mission and you are well on your way to paying off the War Axe. Only another three hundred and seven like that and you'll own it outright."

"Say what?" Terry raised one eyebrow.

Nathan maintained a dead-pan expression. "Just keep plugging away and you'll be living the good life, retired on a Caribbean island."

"Already did that. It's exhausting." Terry rubbed the stubble on his face. "I need to put this one to bed." He pointed to Char. "And then check on my people. You know the status—one lost, one severely injured."

"General Reynolds has sent Ted and a research group from R2D2 to Keeg Station for security reasons. We've received too much intel that suggests the facility is a prime target for undesirables. Ted seemed indifferent, but Felicity was ecstatic, or so I hear. She's also going to be the station manager. The last one died in a bar fight with an Asplesian."

"What's an Asplesian?" Terry mumbled.

"You'll find out. I'm sure Felicity won't put up with any of their crap."

"The old team, back together already. I like it. I'm sure Ted and our Crooner will get along like old buds," Terry suggested.

"It looks to me like warfighting suits you, TH." Nathan waved a handful of papers in front of the camera. "I've sent a batch of RFPs, requests for proposals, your way. Take a look and see what grabs you. They all need the Bad Company yesterday."

Nathan and Terry both shook their heads as they looked at the image of the other.

"Will do, when I can see to read the words, Nathan. All I have to say is fuck those guys, and fuck the next bunch too, whoever they may be."

"Truer words were never spoken. Until then, Terry Henry. Thank you for a job well done."

What matters is that you finish the story. 'Perfect' is the enemy of 'good enough.' Remember that your readers will determine if it's a product worth buying. I want to please my dad because he's one of my biggest fans, but I have a lot of other fans, too. Stay true to the story you establish up front and your way ahead will remain clear.

That should also tell you why I am fanatical about getting that first chapter correct. If you do that, then the rest of the book is a done deal. All that's left is to spend the butt-time in chair to get the words down, which is easier if you already know what you need to accomplish and that your characters have an end point.

Do it now! I am not a fan of starting a rewrite halfway through a draft. I have gone to the extent of sending the first half to my beta readers to see if it worked. Every single time, they said that it did. They asked a couple questions that helped me remove a misleading subplot or better, expand it because they saw it as something that I did not. When readers help you write your story, it is a magical thing.

Abandoning a story. If you cannot get into your book, set it aside. I would never recommend completely abandoning a story. All words are hard to come by. Even if you're churning out 7000 of them a day, they are words well-earned.

I put Become a Successful Indie Author aside for six months because fiction is my moneymaker, but I never abandoned this guide. I kept adding ideas here and there as I thought of things before going back to the novel I was working on at the time. The end result? Become a Successful Indie Author is a fairly decent body of work. Also, the additional time helped me to learn more and add both more and better material.

Out of all of that, I would say that you shouldn't start a book that you are waffling about. If you can write the first and last chapters, then you can write the whole book. Some things may change and you will have to tweak or even rewrite the last chapter, but tell the story. Let the words flow from start to finish.

Don't be an author with a hard drive full of incomplete stories. Be the author with a nice backlist of material for fans to dig into.

Detail Tracking

How do you keep track of your world-building details? The best way you can.

From my business consulting days, I am a huge fan of spreadsheets, so I have all of my business in one massive master spreadsheet. I don't recommend this for those who aren't spreadsheet-savvy, but you do need to keep track somehow. For my Free Trader series, I had columns labeled "Terms," "City/Geography," "People," and "Creatures." As it turned out, I ended up drawing a map and using that for my Geography, but I still needed the spreadsheet to keep track of who the key players were in each of the towns/locations. I had some unique terminology and made a mini-dictionary of terms. The two lengthiest columns, chock-full of entries, were People and Creatures.

My Free Trader series is space opera/space adventure. It is all about the people and the sentient creatures. I wrote about the species and then a short narrative for the history. I added to it as I went with named creatures and named people. Just enough to know that someone was blue-eyed, or had a mate, or some other identifying characteristic. You love your characters, but you're going to forget the little details. In my Nomad series, Simmons in Book 1 became Timmons in Book 2 and all that followed. We caught it after Book 6 was published when someone listened to the audio where it was obvious. It was too late at that point, so we owned the mistake.

It happens. But try to minimize that by keeping a good record. For the Terry Henry Walton Chronicles, I had a single two-column spreadsheet. "Item" and "Definition." That was only okay. I needed more detail. Maybe break out into antagonists, protagonists, and geography. It was a mess of notes and that's how Simmons becomes Timmons. I wrote the books quickly, one after another, but that only partially made the difference.

Maps are key. If you can draw a map or draw on a map, then your world becomes three-dimensional. Yellow stickies can be your friend, until you've got a pile of them falling everywhere. I write military science fiction so I also built organizational charts, because, command and control, of course!

I also built a family tree, since the kids were going to grow up and become integral to the story. We were filling a one hundred and fifty year gap in the timeline, so the family tree was an important overlay of the timeline. That also helped with character interaction between storylines. And all of that stuff was rough and hand-drawn. I tried an online program called Story Shop and that didn't do it for me. It was like trying to manage an Access database where you had to have your linkages correct otherwise you wouldn't find your data.

A couple wonderful friends built a concordance, an alphabetized index of all the words within your book, and it is something you can do for yourself. You load all your books into it and can then search by a variety of phrases to see where each of the references show up. In longer works, this helps your consistency and references, so you don't misplace a bar or put a space station in the wrong solar system. Do a Google search on Concordance Software Download and you'll find some from reputable download sites like CNet.

I don't know about you, but I like the visuals, so I have really rough hand-drawn stuff. I've been able to maintain eight unique points of view (POVs) throughout an entire novel with that level of notetaking. That's also a benefit to writing fast. Had I taken a month off in the middle, I would have lost all train of thought on that book, which is my second-highest reviewed book on Amazon. The complexity of the POVs was important for the story and the readers stayed on board throughout. Many did not put the book down from start to finish because they wanted to know what happened to the next group, and then the next, and so on until the story was told.

When all is said and done, if your world is JRR Tolkien complex, then you need to take your time to make sure all the threads tie together. He took a long time before he released those books because the world-building was at the highest level.

Look to the DragonRiders of Pern. Anne McCaffrey did some incredible world-building, but the readers were introduced to it, one small piece at a time. I modeled my Free Trader in this style—still working to get to Anne's level of prose—and it was easy to build the world as I went, filling in my spreadsheet one passage at a time.

This method worked for me because I had already built the world in my mind, but had I tried to get it all down, then it would have taken time and I would have wrestled with details that held no relevance. Is it ten steps up to the front door or fourteen? Don't worry about it, unless it matters to the story. "He looked up at the door, never taking his eyes from it as he climbed the stairs."

Open the world one door at a time so the reader can process it more easily. Keep in mind that everything you do is for the reader. If you write too complex for an average reader to follow, your market narrows and you'll get some bad reviews. That doesn't make it a bad thing, but I still can't read Tolkien's Silmarillion. I have a law degree, for Pete's sake, but that's more braining than I'm willing to invest in a story where I just want to get away for a while. The Hobbit and Lord of the Rings were perfectly epic or epically perfect, as it may be.

TWO

CREATING YOUR BRAND (YOUR PERSONA)

- What is your brand?
- Building your Email List
- Newsletter
- Other Ways to Have People Follow You
- Selling Books at a Convention
- Pen Name

What is your brand?

"Successful Author" isn't a brand. Success is the result of good writing, publishing, and marketing, but also goes to your brand.

Look at the product logos around you—Nike, the NFL, Dow, Tupperware, Pampered Chef, and so many more. How do you feel when you hear these brands? Now think about authors. What do you think when someone says, "JK Rowling." I surely don't think "that's the Harry Potter woman." I think class and grace, who writes a gripping tale, intricate but for a young audience. I don't know about you, but I want to be more like her, not for the money, but for how she always carries herself and continues to work to spread the Harry Potter brand.

Many of the old-school authors do not have a social media presence. They never needed it because the traditional publishing houses kept their names and books in front of people at the brick and mortar stores, on newsstands, in grocery stores, and in mailers.

We don't live in that world anymore. I saw an article that said 73% of Americans are on Facebook. Most people have an email address. Digital is now. As for tomorrow, who knows what the future holds?

Getting your ads into magazines will reach some old-school readers, but getting your face in front of the digital crowd is instantaneous and far-reaching. We now have worldwide reach! If I publish a book today, it will be available around the world. Think about that and watch the royalties roll in from all of the different Amazon stores.

As long as people get you. Back to your brand.

Don't be a dick, whether to other authors, to your readers, to anyone. I'm not sure how much I can emphasize this. Abrasive people generally don't do well. Being an indie is about doing everything yourself, being alone as you write, but you aren't alone. You are a member of a select group, budding professional authors, people paid for what they write. We all need help, and if you're a dick, people generally won't help you. Don't let your brand harm you.

Be kind, help other folks, especially when you're just starting out. Even though you think you're too new and don't know enough to help others out, you aren't. You can test read or simply be a sounding board to support another new author starting out.

I wrote a couple different post-apocalyptic series, one that had a significant prepper/survivalist slant. The readers in that group have a certain characteristic, just like readers in most other groups. When you appeal to multiple groups, that's when you have to take great care with your brand.

A friend of mine told me that I was a cool Libertarian. I'm not big on labels like conservative or liberal. I believe people are far more complex than that. That's part of my brand—I welcome all people equally. My main characters are couples, equal partners facing antagonists of all shapes and sizes. The themes in my stories run the gamut of social issues. My bottom line is my brand. Peace and justice.

I post on Facebook on multiple pages—I tried to keep my personal page separate from my author page separate from my series page. Everyone friends me on my personal page. It has become the one place for everything. I don't get to rant about politics or religion or the myriad of other issues out there that could be divisive. Many authors do, so understand, that becomes part of your brand. It can also earn an author a bunch of one-star reviews by taking a public stance on a so-called private page. Some multi-million dollar authors are very public about divisive issues. Me? I can't afford to lose a bunch of sales, so I'll remain in the wings. My author career is front and center. Want to know my views on stuff? Let's sit down and enjoy a burger, drink a good dark beer, and talk. Outside of that, my books are my brand. Bottom line, don't hurt your brand with negativity or divisive nonproductive issues.

Do you have a logo? Giveaways? A mark that carries over to every cover?

Think about the DragonLance covers. When you looked at those books, you instantly knew what they were. Do you have a similar typography across a single series? What about all of your books?

Most of mine are similar with a block type font for my name. My series are all easily identifiable as being in the same series. Making bookmarks for giveaways uses the same font setup. It helps to have the same artist do all the typography work. If you are capable of doing your own, even better. I am not, so it's easier for me to be mindful of the brand as I look at new work compared to the old and put it all together.

I'll include my coverwall on the next page so you can see how the brand works across a number of different series.

My Cygnus Space Opera was going to be my magnum opus, but that was before I started writing the Terry Henry Walton Chronicles.

I had a logo done for Cygnus and was contemplating challenge coins, but I put all that on hold because Terry Henry Walton took off like a Titan rocket. The fans wanted more so I gave them more. Everything else went on the backburner.

And that's why I say nothing sells the last book like the next book. The coins and branded goods can all come after there is a following, a market for them. If you put them first, you risk the spend without the return. Despite the fact that every book is your baby, they are still products, and getting a return on your investment is important. Making money from your efforts changes self-publishing from a hobby to a profession.

And what a profession it can be. When there is a demand for branded products outside of our books, then you can create your own low-cost product line. Places like Society6 do print-on-demand where there are no upfront costs. Other places have a minimal setup charge and then they print on demand. Business card printers can do bookmarks by the gross.

What do you put on them, though? Your brand. Let it be all that you are. For those who know me, I share as much knowledge as I have through social media engagement, interviews, and conferences. I'll tell you everything I know for free. My Free Trader series? I love that brand. What about Nomad? Alaska? People associate those with me. That's when you know you have a brand that resonates.

Building Your Email List

When building your email list, there's nothing better than organic—people who have read your book and want more! They sign up because you've put a link in your back matter—the notes at the end of your book. They sign up because they want to know when your next books come out. Keep these folks on a separate list or highlighted in some way.

They are far different from other signups.

I would rate the quality of signups as follows and much of it is based on your target audience when you promote your listbuilder. If you target only readers in your genre with ads, without bleed-over to low-quality freebie seekers, then you will get higher quality signups.

5-Star
Organic signup from your back matter (from your full-length book)

4-Star
Multi-Author Anthology where each contributor writes an original story and they are consolidated into a single book that the authors share with their lists only (not a general promotion - a genre-aligned effort)
Short story giveaway (they signed up to get your short story for free – this is only you giving it away).

3-Star
Sign up from personal contact (book signing). I would have thought these would be higher, but I've done four different events and can't tell you a single person from those who is still on my list.

2-Star
General promotions across all genres with a giveaway of some sort. These are 30 or 40 author consolidated freebies where one signup adds the person to 30 or 40 different lists, even though the reader gets a comparable number of stories.

1-Star
Big giveaway (a Kindle or a computer where they have to sign up to your list to enter)

I don't have a zero star as there is potential to find your next superfan in all of these efforts. The 1-Star promotions could add tens of thousands of names to your list, which can get expensive, depending on your newsletter list provider. I use MailChimp because of its interface and ease of use. MailerLite is about half the cost, but comes with its own challenges. Regardless. A list with 30,000 names can be expensive to maintain, especially if those 30,000 don't buy your stuff.

The reason for your list is to inform your fans about you, about new releases, about other authors you like. There are a wide variety of engagements.

Newsletter

This is a direct link to your readers. The newsletter is your hedge against any release strategy. You don't need an algorithm b[...] other advertising with your fans. You tell them that your latest [...] is available and they buy it. You don't have to go looking for them.

I know there are successful people without newsletters. The[y] engage their fans in a different way, through a blog or some other vehicle, but they invest the time in keeping their fans informed. A blog is a pull effort in that you need the fans to check your blog as part of their online routine, which means that you need to keep the content fresh. That's a great deal of effort that can be rewarding.

I think sending a newsletter is so much easier. I've tried blogging with regularity and it was draining. I had about 300 people a day stop by and visit, but it took a Facebook post telling them that there was a new blog post. You will lose a certain percentage of readers (I've heard 30%) for every additional link they have to click. I figured that I'd simply keep them informed on Facebook and if they clicked the picture, it took them directly to the Amazon product page. One click and they were in a position to buy.

Same thing for my newsletter—subscribers can click on the picture on links below the picture. I include two—one that goes directly to the US store and a universal link (I use Booklinker) that will take a subscriber to the appropriate store for where they are (Amazon UK, Amazon DE, whatever, keeping in mind that I am currently exclusive to Amazon with all my stuff).

I start off every newsletter with a personal bit. Welcome from the Sub-Arctic! I learned that one from Mark Dawson. It is exotic if you don't live in the far north, I mean really far north, one hundred and fifty miles from the Arctic Circle. In the winter, it's cold and dark, and in the summer, we have twenty-four hours of daylight. It's different. I share pictures of moose in the yard or snow well over my dog's head.

And then I go into my pitch. My main book first—on sale, today only! Or something like that, then freebies from other folks or discounted books. A new thing I do is look for discounts on books

n genres. I look for anything on sale from
 lre Norton. If I find something, I list it with
 lenty of clicks, which also tells me that my
 aligned with that genre and those authors,
 et my ad campaigns.
 ith a laundry list of my books. I had to go
 g as it is extensive. That was a recommen-
ᴗy James Baldwin, who has been a significant help with my newsletters and overall graphics.

For those who are wide, you can list all the stores where your book is available. I think those lists of links look far more profound.

Back to the newsletter. How do you do it?

I'm not going to go through a step-by-step sequence for a specific provider, but here's what I do to give something away.

1. Write a good short story or provide the first few chapters of your full-length book. (If you intend to go Amazon exclusive using Kindle Direct Publishing Select, then you can give away 10% of your book without violating the exclusivity clause in the Terms of Service, as of this writing anyway.) It's important that this work is a good representative of you and your writing. This is the face that you will present to potential fans.
2. Format it well. Make sure you include quality front matter, the words at the beginning of the book with your copyright and what that story or book is about and why—the why and the opportunity to sign up for your newsletter up front is important as many people stop reading as soon as the story is over. Make it easy for people to sign up.
3. Load the material onto a site like BookFunnel or Instafreebie, making sure you check the box for mandatory email collection. If you can't set it for mandatory email collection, then you will get fewer

subscribers, but they will probably be higher quality. It's a tradeoff.
4. Make sure it's active. I have multiple email accounts and have signed up for my own newsletter multiple times with all of them. Do not ever deliver a bad experience to your potential readers, either through a typo-infested bad story or through an avoidable technical glitch. You are trying to turn a potential reader into a fan and then into a buyer.
5. Use a service like MailChimp—there are dozens out there to choose from, some are easier than others, but that usually comes at a higher cost—which will compile email addresses from other signups, integrated from BookFunnel, for example.

I have direct links to the MailChimp signup from my webpage as well as from my Facebook page as well as in the back matter of all my books.

Funnel the new emails through your on-boarding sequence. I use three emails. The first one welcomes them aboard and offers a free download. The second one has nothing for sale and is simply me talking about me, without too much me. The third one offers my Martelle Starter Library for $2.99, which has three full-length novels and a short story. This is where people are introduced to me as a seller of books.

Derek Murphy is a newsletter master and his automation sequence has twelve emails. I don't have that kind of patience. Check out Derek's work on the subject if you want more insight into how he does it. He carefully cultivates how he brings people on board, shifting them into various groups based on their level of engagement through the on-boarding process. It really is masterful. It also allows for a slower release because he has his readers and potential readers on the hook, waiting for his next book.

They aren't going anywhere. As long as they are still subscribed, ach out and touch them, let them know about your life, your latest release, or just about anything that ...ted with them as readers.

...ou don't cultivate a readership that only stays on ...ard to get free stuff.

Giving books away for free is a marketing strategy. Use it for that. If you give all your books away for free, you will collect readers who aren't willing to pay for your stuff. If you want to make a living as a writer, you need readers willing to pay for your stories. Occasionally, I will run promotions to give away the first book in a series. With read-through/buy-through to the second and later books, I make good money, earning a positive return on investment. I never give away later books in the series, although that could also be a marketing strategy. Use it wisely.

I keep applying for a BookBub-featured deal offering some of my other titles for free, like the 6th book in a series. It can stand alone, although it's best to be read in order. But with BookBub, it is more than worth it. They can put my book in front of a quarter of a million science fiction readers. I don't need very many to give me a shot as I have an extensive backlist. Backlist is where good money can be found, but I also say that nothing sells the last book like the next book.

This is what it takes. It all starts with connecting with your readers.

A newsletter makes it possible to have a single release a year and not lose your readership. If you're releasing every month, then they know you're there. The readers won't have forgotten you. I target whale readers, those who read multiple books every week. They can read far faster than I can write, but when I bring a new whale reader on board, they plow through my backlist, and that's good for about $50. One reader. Forty or more books.

They say it's easier to sell ten books to one person than one book to ten different people. We keep working toward both—ten books to ten different readers. That is the golden archway to success, then ten more, and ten more.

Other ways to have people follow you

Amazon allows followers. The only drawback with Amazon is that you have no idea exactly how many or who they are. You don't contact them about your new release, Amazon does. Amazon knows marketing so trust that they'll get the word out, unless no one ever clicks on those links, then you have a different issue.

I've run a huge number of giveaways with my books, other books in my genre, and even a Kindle Paperwhite. All of it was dedicated to have people follow me as part of the giveaway. I think that I have thousands. I focused the giveaway specifically toward readers in my genre, although that may have been narrow-sighted. Since Amazon maintains the list and it doesn't cost anything, it doesn't hurt for them to cast the net far and wide.

If you let Amazon pimp it out for you as part of the giveaway, you'll get a bunch of freebie seekers and such, but how can that be bad if you never know who they are or have to pay for them? Amazon knows marketing. Trust them to get your stuff in front of people who just may buy your books.

BookBub will issue new release alerts. The good news about BookBub is that you can see exactly how many people are following you. When they send out the new release alert, it looks a lot like a Featured Deal. That's where people go to buy books.

I recommend including a BookBub follow link in your back matter, along with your newsletter signup, Amazon author page, and then add in your social media links.

Facebook, Twitter, Instagram, and whatever other ones out there can be lucrative, but like a blog or your newsletter, they take effort. I post something on Facebook every single day, usually multiple times a day. I'll boost my author posts to make sure they get visibility in front of my author followers.

For Facebook, I have my personal page which has devolved into me being an author page, so I no longer have a personal page. I have an Author Craig Martelle page, which is good because I can run ads from there. I also have a Terry Henry Walton page, the main character in my biggest selling series. But the group page that I have for fans allows them to post and readily be seen by other members. The other pages do not. This is important for fan interaction.

There are pros and cons for each type of page you maintain on Facebook. My personal page gets great visibility, but I can't advertise from there. My author page has been constrained by FB algos, so I have to pay to get some posts in front of potential buyers/future superfans. My group page allows for great interaction, but I can't advertise from there. Positives and negatives everywhere. I haven't found the best place for FB one-stop shopping, but I'll keep working it through multiple angles.

I haven't used Twitter or Instagram in a long time, but if you are a big user and also write books, you should be able to blend the two. This goes back to your brand. If people know you and like you, when you tell them that you have a book available, they'll be more welcoming. If all you ever tell them is things about your book, you may find them resistant.

Your brand. Make it a good one.

Selling Books at a Convention

I did two years hawking my books at ICON, a show in Cedar Rapids—the largest scifi convention in Iowa. They tout 500 attendees. I lost money by doing that show, but I got a tax-deductible trip back to see my old man (he's 82), so I went a couple times. Here is what I've learned.

1. Make your table 3-dimensional so it will catch people's eyes.

- Colors are good
- Banners help
- Book stacks look impressive (people will buy the first in a

series, so bring more of those and fewer of the later volumes)
- I'm hand-carrying all my stuff from Alaska so will be limited on what I can bring. If you're driving, you could bring more books and a self-standing banner, and things like that
- I gained some hardcore fans from last year's show
- Bring a convention admin pack—duct tape, clothespins, stapler, pens, paperclips, stuff like that. You may not need them, but might get an in with someone who does.

2. I have candy on my table, so people stop. That helps me start a conversation. "You like scifi?" (A safe question. It was a scifi show.) Mix hard candy and soft candy, maybe even some sugar-free.

3. Bring bookmarks and business cards. This is your brand—get them to take one with them.

- I have a BookFunnel link on my business cards for a free short story download with mandatory opt-in to my newsletter (NL)
- A new idea (thanks, 20Books!)—bring a tablet (Galaxy, iPad, Kindle Pro, even your smart phone) with a simple NL signup link. People can type in their email right at the table
- A separate sheet of paper with your book blurbs. Make it one page so someone can pick it up and take it with them. (An attendee suggested this last year as they wanted to read my book descriptions but had too many sessions to go to and didn't have the time to read the back of each book.)

4. Make sure you take credit cards.

- I use my phone and one person went to sign and said,

"Oh, that's dirty!" Bring alcohol screen wipes to keep your signing device clean, whether it is a phone, tablet, whatever

- Have change in case people pay in cash—assume everyone is going to pay with a $20. I price all my books at $10 for the show.
- I also had to get an Iowa business license just for the show, so I could collect tax. I add the tax for CC transactions but not for cash deals

5. I stand the entire time. I greet everyone as they come by. They gave me the first table inside the entrance to the show the first year. It was premier. The convention organizer was very pleased with my presence and gave me that same spot the second year, too. I am an introvert by nature, but reciting easy phrases and such takes the edge off. It's okay. When they pick up a book, you can look at the book together, not each other. That's easier.

6. I also did a panel the second year on self-publishing. We only had five people show up to the panel, but they were fully engaged because they wanted to become authors.

Remember, you are your brand. You must be cordial and accommodating. One attendee last year told me my books were crap—in a very loud voice—because they were 6x9 format. I had no comeback to that besides telling him that I'd consider going smaller. Guess who showed up at my table the second year to look at my smaller books?

Half of them were 5x8. He nodded in appreciation, but didn't buy a book. That is also a lesson. When people are that vocal about demanding accommodation, they probably are looking for an excuse on not being accommodated.

I talked with other vendors and authors. I have a great deal more experience now, so my conversations with the others will be more robust and less fangirlish. (Glen Cook and Joe Haldeman attend each year.)

Would I go back? No. I have no interest in selling at conventions as that is not my business model. Going to conventions to speak on panels is something completely different. Having bookmarks and business cards to give away no matter where you go is important. Glad-handing and being present are important, as you never know the person you'll meet.

Joe Haldeman walked past my table, but a shiny thing across the aisle drew him away before I could engage. I hunted him down later to introduce myself and say a few kind words, but I could have done that without standing behind my table not selling books for three days. I sold $250 worth, but the margin was low, so I didn't even pay for my food, let alone my hotel room and plane ticket. For me, the hassle of doing the show wasn't worth it. For some of the local authors who didn't have to pay for travel, food, or lodging, they did pretty well, both in exposure and sales.

Understand, from a business perspective, what your goals are. I would rather be on more panels and spend the time talking with people than trapped behind a table. You show that you know what you're talking about by talking about the business of self-publishing.

Pen Name

If you have a pen name to keep your personal life separate from your published life, you have to do everything above separately. Sometimes, keeping a pen name is a good idea. Many erotica writers use pen names. I would if I wrote in that genre because I wouldn't want my dad, my biggest fan, running across it. I don't have the energy to manage multiple personalities, so I use my real name.

Stalkers and internet trolls have made pen names more attractive, too, in order for the author to fly under the radar.

If you have multiple pen names, then you are looking at multiple personas, multiple brands. Understand the workload before you take it on. I am good with sticking in one genre. I don't have to worry about who did what or who knows which person I am at the moment.

· · ·

You are your brand in everything you do. Some people are successful in separating their private life from their public life. I failed miserably at that and ended up changing the public perception of my private life, then I only had to maintain one persona at all times. I have a single website, a single author page, and multiple Facebook pages that all have the same theme regarding me.

THREE

THE BUSINESS-SIDE OF BEING AN AUTHOR

- Defining Success
- Where does the data come from?
- Expenses and Revenue
- Organizing your business so you have a place to put that revenue and deduct those expenses
- Tracking Data
- Organizing your business is about managing risk
- SWOT Analysis of Your Business
- Sphere of Control - Sphere of Influence
- Representative Business Structure by Joe Solari
- Managing Your Taxes
- Taxes
- Copyright & Keeping Your Books Safe

Defining Success

I can't make you a successful indie author. Only you can do that because only you have *your* definition of success.

Not everyone gets to be successful in the indie business. In the

Marine Corps, I heard someone defend another Marine saying that if he got punished for a transgression, it would hurt his career. The answer? Not everyone gets a career in the Corps. Less than 10% who start out make it the full 20 years.

Most authors (traditional and indie) make less than $10,000 a year. There are things you can do to improve your chances, like working hard on the right things. It won't take long to vault past those at the top of the bell curve in regards to revenue, move from average to above average.

Is revenue your goal? Is it simply publishing and having strangers read and like your book? All of that is possible if you believe.

Work first on your goal. Make it achievable, something that you can do in the next month. Write it down and stick it on your monitor, your refrigerator or wherever you will often look. Focus on achieving that goal. When you've hit it, put the old goal in a box and post a new goal. This is your ladder to success. But what's at the top? For many, it's to be able to write full-time. That is in a distant cloud, but that doesn't mean you can't get there. It only means that the ladder is long and has a great number of steps.

And work. Never doubt that there will be work involved and not all of it is as sexy as writing a killer story!

That's my segue to the business side of managing your author business.

As an indie, you are responsible for all of it. If you make great money but don't pay your taxes, there's only one person who gets the blame. If you don't keep track of your expenses and have trouble finding them in order to deduct them, there's only one person to blame.

If you gasp in horror, then you need to step back, take a deep breath, and understand that you can do this. If you have the ability to write a book, you can manage your own author business.

There are two main things to be aware of in everything you do: Revenue and Expenses. That's the bottom line of all business. I'll also talk about cash flow, because the money you make today won't get paid for a while, while the money you spend today is gone today.

Where does the data come from?

Where will you get data that matters? I won't be flippant and say from everywhere, because it's not funny and it's not true.

At this point in the book, I will tell you that nearly all of my experience is exclusive to Amazon. That is where my experience lies and where I make most of my money.

In Amazon, your primary source of raw data regarding your sales is from the KDP Dashboard. They show pseudo-real time data in two charts. (If you are not in Kindle Unlimited, it's one chart.) You can get add-on software packages that do a better job of displaying the data from your KDP dashboard. I use BookReport, but there are many others out there like Trackerbox, Akreport, and ReaderLinks. I've heard great things about ReaderLinks and I may have to try it out at some point, because it supposedly will import your AMS data, too.

I also use Excel by downloading the data and parsing it myself, although the data presentation changes often enough that one needs to be an Excel power user in order to keep it working. I am a power user, but it still takes time to redo the formulas.

AMS gives you data that you can download. Brian Meeks will tell you to download that data every single day to compare it against the previous day in order to keep yourself up to date.

I use BookReport because it tells me enough of what I need. Here's what the start of a new day looks like for me. Made a few bucks—total on the day is at the top—and then the covers from highest earning to lowest.

And then the pie chart of the breakdown. You'll see in the next screen that the differentiation is minimal. No breakdown data on ads, so I'll check AMS and Facebook Ads Manager to see what kind of impressions I'm getting.

CRAIG MARTELLE

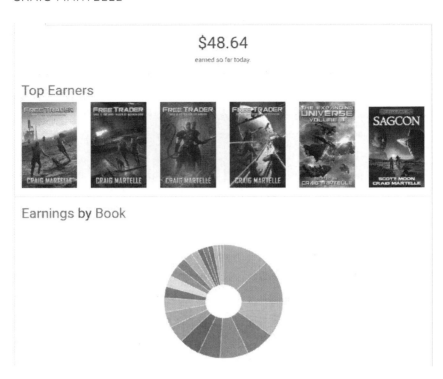

ASIN	Earnings	Sales	Pages	~Borrows	KU Royalties	Sales Royalties
Totals	$53.88	2	10,480	39	$48.29	$5.58
The Free Trader of Warren Deep	$7.23	0	1,126	3	$5.25	$1.98
Southern Discontent	$6.26	0	918	4	$4.22	$2.04
Battle for the Amazon	$5.81	0	1,239	3	$5.81	$0.00
The Expanding Universe 3: Space Opera, Military SciFi, Space Adventure, & Alien Contact!	$5.17	1	955	1	$4.01	$1.16
Adventures on RV Traveler	$4.01	0	861	2	$4.01	$0.00
SAGCON: Assignment Darklanding Book 06	$2.87	0	616	4	$2.87	$0.00
Free Trader on the High Seas	$2.74	0	587	1	$2.74	$0.00
The Free Trader of Planet Vii	$2.47	0	561	1	$2.47	$0.00
Cygnus Expanding: Humanity Fights for Freedom	$2.36	0	506	1	$2.36	$0.00
Free the North!	$2.05	0	430	1	$2.05	$0.00
Cruiseliner Hades 7: A Lost 77 Worlds Tale	$1.74	1	287	2	$1.34	$0.40

This is how I have my BookReport set up to run. I tell it to use last month's KU payout rate for the estimate. Many people set it at $0.004 in order to low-ball the estimate. You know yourself. If you think you are making more, do you tend to spend more? As of this writing, KU has not gone below .004, so that is fairly safe for a low-end estimate. You can look at everything above that as gravy.

If you want the raw data, here's where you get that. This is on your kdp.amazon.com page when you click "Reports."

The default view is the Sales Dashboard. Is there any doubt when my release dates are? If you scroll to the bottom of that page, you'll find the Generate Report button. Also take a close look—you'll see that what this report shows as royalties does not match what BookReport shows. It won't. BookReport pulls the data from the generated report and includes the page reads, which Amazon does not include for a royalties calculation. They don't even fathom a guess because they don't want to be liable.

Marketplace	Currency	eBook Royalty	Paperback Royalty	Total Royalty
Amazon.com	USD	25.63	0.00	25.63
Amazon.co.uk	GBP	1.16	0.00	1.16
Amazon.de	EUR	0.29	0.00	0.29
Amazon.fr	EUR	0.00	0.00	0.00
Amazon.es	EUR	0.00	0.00	0.00
Amazon.it	EUR	0.00	0.00	0.00
Amazon.nl	EUR	0.00	0.00	0.00
Amazon.co.jp	JPY	0.00	0.00	0.00
Amazon.in	INR	0.00	0.00	0.00
Amazon.ca	CAD	0.35	0.00	0.35
Amazon.com.br	BRL	0.00	0.00	0.00
Amazon.com.mx	MXN	0.00	0.00	0.00
Amazon.com.au	AUD	0.00	0.00	0.00

If you collaborate and aren't the one who published the book, Amazon and BookReport won't show you that data. Everything I have here is minus twenty-five of my bestselling books. BookReport at one time considered sharing, but that idea never came to fruition. I would love to have all of my numbers in one place. I do, but that is in my very fragile and phenomenally complex Excel spreadsheet. I won't share it because it breaks on me, so wouldn't be much use to anyone, not even another super-user, because they would spend less time recreating the formulas than trying to follow the logic from mine.

I also gather data from ACX (audiobooks), CreateSpace (paperbacks), Amazon Affiliate program (sending people to Amazon from my web page), and my traditional publisher (I have four books with them and they give me a quarterly report in Excel). This data is very broad, as in gross sales only. I check each day as I run ads trying to push my audiobooks. That is a tough nut to crack, but we're working on some things to give them a big push.

I also get data from a few collaborators. When I incorporate their data that applies to me, I have tens of thousands of lines of raw numbers. The good news is that if you have that many numbers, you already know how to work with them or can hire people to do it for you because you are making good money.

Amazon also keeps a great deal of data secret from the author. How many people have borrowed my book? You have to estimate that from your author ranking. Here's what I've come up with, totally unscientifically but based on my releases and author ranks and talking with those who have put books into the top 100. You see that I have two columns for number of sales because it is harder to get the rank in the first place than it is to hold the rank. Amazon averages book sales and rewards those that have consistently high sales, not those with spikes. Having a solid week of good sales is better than a single stellar day as far as book ranking goes.

This chart is a guesstimate. If you release your best book ever and BookBub rewards you with a Featured Deal and you sell 5001 copies on the same day that JK Rowling releases a new Harry Potter book and a new Jack Reacher book hits and Steven King delivers his best book ever, you may not be number one. Everything here is subject to what every other author on Amazon is doing, and that includes the big five traditional publishers. Sometimes, you don't want to try and outspend them. Sit back, watch, and jump in when they are done playing. It doesn't take long.

Kindle Rank	Estimate of Books Sold and Borrowed in one day	Daily Sales & Borrows to maintain rank
1	5000	5000
5	3500	2500
10	2500	200
50	1500	1000
100	1000	500
200	500	300
1000	200	100
2500	100	50
5000	75	25
10,000	50	15
50,000	2	2
100,000	1	1

Your author rank is another number that is almost completely meaningless except as a general barometer of sales numbers. That's it. Don't dwell on that too much. As you sell more books, your rank will increase and rank is mostly irrelevant outside of the top 20,000 to 30,000, because sales of a few books one way or another will create wild swings in rank. I celebrated like a wild man when I first made it into the top 100,000, then the top 50k, and then into the top 10k.

Each level is a new plateau from which you launch higher and higher. I feel successful because it's been more than a year since I've been out of the top 100 science fiction authors. I've been out of the top 1000 for a total of maybe 45 days in the past year as well. Commensurately, sales have been good.

One of the lies of your author rank is that it is purely based on sales and borrow numbers (not profit). An author could be spending a great deal on advertising, so much so that they are losing money because all their books are 99 cents. They may have a great rank, but are heading toward bankruptcy. That's not what you want. Don't sacrifice your profitability for the fleeting number that is your author rank.

This is your business. Let your ego be driven by your artistic side, but let your business be run by the cold numbers person. Make a profit and make this a viable business. If you get your author rank when your books are at full price, then you'll be able to afford business retreats in Bali...

Revenue

I watch my KDP dashboard. You can watch your D2D dashboard too, as well as Kobo or any others where you have titles for sale. Understand that all numbers are delayed. The numbers you see on all your dashboards are only estimates until they are actually paid.

Amazon pays two months down the road. Traditional publishers may pay six months to one year later. For an indie using Amazon, money earned on Feb 28 will be paid promptly by April 30th. Money earned on March 1st, will be paid by May 31st. Simple as that.

They also convert funds from all other currencies into your preferred payment currency. This will probably result in your earnings being less that what is estimated, but the bottom line and what you get taxed on is what you are actually paid.

But you need those estimates so you can control your spend. If you keep spending more than you're making, that money will have to come from somewhere. Beginning with a warchest of funds is good, but not always possible. Barry Hutchison showed how he could launch a book without spending a penny and without spending any of his own money. He didn't start running ads until the money was actually in the bank. He didn't pay for covers or editing. There are ways and if you want to learn how Barry did it, you can watch his presentation from 20Books London called "Bookstrapping" on YouTube.

Organizing your business so you have a place to put that revenue and deduct those expenses

If you don't make a profit two years out of five (at last count from the IRS), then your business is a hobby and the IRS will tax the income from it, but won't let you deduct the expenses. So, earn a damn profit for at least two years. And then go crazy and keep earning a profit.

Setting up your author business before you publish

- Get an Employer Identification Number (or your country's equivalent). EINs are free to get online. This will separate your social security number from your business accounting.
- Get a business checking account. This will be a separate account to manage all your business finances. Sometimes, you'll need your company established to do this. Then get a debit card for the account. You may not be able to get a line of credit right up front, but I would not encourage getting credit as an author. Sales are not guaranteed, but if you keep track of revenue, then you will have an idea of what you'll be paid in a couple months.
- Start a business. You don't need to do this, but your state may require it to start a business bank account. You can set up an S Corporation, which is usually the least expensive and least time-consuming of the options. This also means getting your business license. That's how my state works anyway.
- Set aside enough working capital to be able to pay for your author business needs. It could be as little as $1000, but you need something. You can publish at no cost, but remember, we want you to treat this as a business from the outset and you need to manage your cash flow.
- Build your business tracking spreadsheet. I always recommend using Excel (or Google Sheets or something like that).

- Establish a social media presence. You will want your own website. The separate website helped me get my business checking account. Facebook, Twitter, and Instagram are free, and you'll want to build your presence on one or all. Depends on what kind of time you have. I only use FB, as that is where over 50% of my fans can be found.
- Remember: Dress for the job you want. If you want to be taken seriously as an author, you have to act like a professional, have a professional presence, and keep striving to get better at all aspects of your self-publishing business.

As soon as you publish your book and put a price tag on it, your book has become a product for sale. This is where you must step back from the personal relationship you have with your creation and look at it dispassionately.

"A book is not just a book." It could be a foundational brick in the building of your business. Make it great, and then make more.

The starving artist isn't a myth. Those artists probably didn't understand the business side of their art, or they sold out to middlemen who took the majority of their earnings because they wanted to focus on only their art.

You're an indie. You don't have that luxury, and you don't want it! There is no sense in paying someone else to do something you can do for yourself, until your writing is bringing in enough income that it's not worth your time to do the businessy stuff yourself. That is a business decision as well because you've looked at your time and seen that your writing hours have a value that exceeds the amount it takes to do the work yourself.

Until you get to that level of revenue, don't be afraid! It's not that hard. Use the checklist to make sure you've covered your bases.

- Establish your business name (I went with Craig Martelle Inc or CMI)
- Get EIN (https://www.irs.gov/businesses/small-businesses-self-employed/apply-for-an-employer-identification-number-ein-online)
- Establish your business (this is State specific – understand the benefits for an S Corp versus an LLC versus a PC or the myriad of other organizations). In Alaska, flow through taxation of a sole proprietorship is an S Corporation. In Arizona, that structure describes an LLC. It is unique to each state.
- Get your business checking account (and point all your payments, Amazon, ACX, CreateSpace/Ingram Spark, etc to it)
- Establish your business presence through a website. Once again, I went with the easiest thing I could think of – craigmartelle.com
- Start tracking your income and expenses

How much business stuff do you need to do? That's a good question. I'll share my daily routine.

1. I download the latest KDP Sales Dashboard and copy the information into my spreadsheet—available from a link in the back of the book.

2. Check my Amazon Marketing Service (AMS) ads for the best impressions/clicks/buys. Adjust as necessary. Low conversion rates get a highlight to update the blurb on that particular book.

3. Check my Facebook (FB) ads for conversion and relevance rating.

4. Check ad copy on my current WIP. I find it best to write the blurb and taglines as I go.

5. Check reviews. Yes, I read all my reviews. Bad reviews mean I'm putting my book into the wrong people's hands. If so, see where

the buyer came from—check their other reviews. Adjust ad targeting (usually FB).

6. On the 15th of the month, I download my KDP Report from Amazon. You'll find that on your KDP Reports page under the Prior Months' Royalties tab.

Tracking Data

How do we use data to make business decisions as indies? That's the real question.

How many of us have BookReport running in the background, so we can hear the cha-ching? I do. I finally stopped looking when it made that noise. It didn't change anything I was doing at the moment. I recommend turning off the cha-ching once you realize that you are a professional author and are making money at this business.

As a business consultant, and specifically a business diagnostics expert, I worked with numerous businesses that collected every nit-noid bit of data and compiled and built massive, all-encompassing reports.

If the data doesn't change anything you do, stop looking at it! At the least, reduce the frequency that you look at the numbers. I hope you are checking your FB ad spend daily as well as your AMS impressions and spend. But hourly? There's no need for that.

BookReport or one of the other after-market data tracking programs? Once a day is sufficient, unless you are looking for a trigger to change something like validating how a promotion or ad campaign is resonating with buyers.

If you can automate something, do it! KDP provides you a full report. You don't need to hand-jam your KENP reads into a separate spreadsheet every day. You can download the spreadsheet from the bottom of your reports page once a week, or however often you need to review your data. The fewer books you have = less often, but that's when you do it the most. I should study the data hard every day, but I only have time to do it once a week. I have some 70 titles earning revenue for me. It's best to stay on top of what is doing what, so be familiar with your top titles and general flavor of your backlist series. I now parse my data by series to give me a better look at how things are doing.

If you collaborate, only the person or entity that published the story will get the data. I can directly access about half of all my data. I am dependent upon Michael Anderle for the other half as he is the one who hits publish on our co-authored titles. He is a very busy person, but will still give me the data daily if I want it to bounce the numbers against an ad campaign that I'm running or for some other purpose. Generally, though, my time is best spent writing the next book and managing the business finances.

Your word count? Track that closely and match it against your realistic goals. That is how you get to "The End." Adjust if you're not hitting those goals. My word count has improved because I shut everything down except the story I'm working on. I take that to the finish line before starting something else. Why would you track word count as part of your business?

Being professional means being able to predict your production. Whether it is one book a year or one book a month, you should be able to know not just what you can do, but what you will do. You might have a co-author opportunity. Winging it with the numbers probably won't fly. It wouldn't with me. I can't take on a co-author who isn't sure what he/she can produce on a regular basis. My business plan doesn't support a nebulous delivery date to build the business.

When it comes to being an indie, you are your own boss. Don't let data overwhelm you. Collect and review the data that will help you manage your business. Everything else? Take a look out of curiosity's sake, but if it doesn't change what you're doing, then why? Don't let data be a distraction. Use it as the tool it is.

Organizing your business is about managing risk

There are a plethora of options out there in how to organize your business, and all of them have their own benefits and pitfalls. It depends on how you best want to manage your risk.

I personally have an S Corporation, copyright my works in my own name, and carry an umbrella policy—also called errors and omissions—for insurance coverage. This works the best for me to limit my tax exposure, while providing risk protection.

The chance of an author getting sued is low, but you have to understand that it is a risk. If you are sued and lose, then if you have no corporate organization or other protections, the lawsuit winner can go after your personal belongings like your home or your vehicle. As a lawyer, I can represent myself, I hope competently. Most people would have to hire an attorney and that can get expensive. Know the triggers and avoid them. Here are a few examples of what not to do.

- Don't use Disney characters in your books
- Don't use song lyrics without permission (unless fair use applies, which is usually limited to non-fiction or satire)
- Don't show a corporation in a bad light (an example would be writing a story where Taco Bell causes a listeria outbreak where hundreds of people die)

How do you avoid those miscues? Google. Find a Taco name that isn't taken. The Taco Place. I just Googled it and there wasn't a taco joint with that name. You can change names, mix things up. As long as you make an effort to not use real company names, you will be far less likely to end up on the wrong end of administrative law.

SWOT Analysis of Your Business

SWOT stands for strengths, weaknesses, opportunities, and threats. It is a business analysis tool. I'll do mine so you can have an idea of how I look at my business world.

Strength – significant production, business savvy with a continuous improvement mindset.

Weakness – I admit it, I don't like marketing and I hate self-promo. I suck so bad when I try to do it that I look like a complete buffoon.

Opportunities – thanks to tools like KDP Rocket, I am comfortable that I'm not only writing in a big market, but that it is still growing for books that resonate. The readers are there, we only need to get a book into their hands.

Threat – there's no outside threat except losing power or something catastrophic happening to my home in the Alaskan wild. The real threat would come from within, either burnout or illness. I'm not completely healthy, but writing is a great outlet for my energy.

Exploit the strengths, minimize the weaknesses, dig into the opportunities, and mitigate the threats. I have not slowed down, but thanks to outlining, I have greatly increased my production without any additional work. I have set aside time each week to run through my ad campaigns, although I usually cut that in half when the time comes. Nothing sells the last book like the next book. Okay, if I market well, I get both victories.

Keep writing in my market while watching the new players. It appears that space fantasy is taking off. My Mystically Engineered short story is resonating. That may be a new market to explore, but I don't have the bandwidth to write it right now.

Sphere of Control - Sphere of Influence

From a business perspective, you are in control of a lot, but not everything, not even a fraction of everything. If you've ever had a title with a traditional publisher, then you'll see what real frustration is as you are in control of almost nothing and have to trust that they'll take of your concerns seriously. My publisher, Permuted Press, has done me right. They are a pleasure to work with and if I have concerns, they address them right away.

If you need to fix a typo in your book, you make the change and upload the new eBook. If you decide you need a new cover, you get a new one and upload it. If you want to change your blurb every single day, you can do that, too.

Changing your blurb – do it out of the KDP bookshelf page (if you're on Amazon) or through D2D if you're wide (I personally would not go direct to other retailers because you have the same learning curve for each – who has time for that?). On Amazon, if you do it through your Author Central page, it's convenient, but if there is a price change or anything like that on your book, it will revert to what you posted through the KDP bookshelf. If you want to dabble, then Author Central works, but if you want to fix things for good, do it through the book's page from the KDP bookshelf.

If you want more sales, you can control the advertising, but you cannot control the buyers. You have to make your product enticing, and that can be partly done through a good cover or a good blurb.

Representative Business Structure by Joe Solari

No matter what advice you receive, from a lawyer or certified public accountant, it comes with the caveat that every circumstance is different and no responsibility is taken for the outcomes if you follow the advice given. Of course the same goes with this article. I can tell you what I think and what I have done and why I think it makes sense.

Joe lives in Illinois and in this state, this is an option for an author's business structure.

Set up a subchapter S corporation.

This is a little more complex than starting an LLC but well within the skill set of anyone who is running an indie publishing shop. The benefits are below:

You can pay yourself a salary and issue a W-2.

. . .

The power of the W-2:
If you are self-employed, you know the pain of not having a W-2. Anytime you go to buy a car or refinance your house and tell the credit manager that you are self-employed, the options for financing are either diminished or expensive. However, if you are able to provide a W-2, you can easily go through standard loan qualification. With an S Corporation, you will be a shareholder, an officer, and an EMPLOYEE. This is impossible with an LLC. This may not seem like a big deal now, but it will be if you attempt to buy something big and need credit.

Reduce Tax Burden
Here is another benefit that is perfectly legal but only available to Subchapter S Corporations.
Since you can now be a salaried employee, your Medicare, FICA, and state employment taxes apply to the salary you make. You will need to adjust your salary in proportion to the overall revenue of the business. The IRS is aware of the trick where an owner takes a low salary to keep employment taxes down. A good rule of thumb is 50% of the operating profits.
The profits of the corporation would typically require you to pay corporate income tax but since you are subchapter S, profits pass through to you and you pay at your personal income level. That means you save the 3-15% self-employment tax that you would pay if you had an LLC!
With a bank account, EIN, and articles of incorporation, you now have all the necessary pieces for operating your publishing business. The first thing to do is switch your KDP and other accounts that provide income to the business to use the business EIN, and then set the funds to go to your business bank account.

. . .

Managing Your Taxes

A good rule of thumb is to set aside 30% of your profit for taxes. A better rule is to set aside 40%.

Make your quarterly estimated tax payments (in the U.S.) and note that they aren't normal quarters. Look to make your payments before these dates.

- April 15
- June 15
- September 15
- January 15

S Corp or individuals should use Form 1040es through the IRS EFTPS portal. LLC & C Corporations will use the Form 941, which is for payroll taxes, unless your LLC uses flow-through taxation.

That stuff makes my brain hurt. Consult a tax professional to get it right, but you have to get it mostly right. If you make money but don't pay quarterly taxes, the IRS could hit you with a penalty. You don't want to give the tax man any more money than you have to.

With the new tax laws (effective for 2018 in the United States), we don't have fidelity yet on what we can and can't deduct, so that will have to be a later supplement. No matter what, keep good records with receipts for every penny you spend. If you can deduct it, then you will need the receipt. If you can't? Well, better safe than sorry.

And the bottom line is to deduct your expenses, you need to make a profit. You can't keep deducting if your business isn't making money. That's one of the main reasons most businesses go out of business in their fourth year, because the old IRS rules required a business to make a profit two years out of five in order to be something more than a hobby. As a hobby, you get taxed on the revenue without the commensurate deduction for expenses. Cool? Not quite. Make a profit. I gave myself one year to get into the black. I did in my eleventh month of self-publishing, although I had a negative carry-over to the second year.

The second year, I made plenty to cover that and add significantly to Uncle Sam's coffers. As I tell those who make it in this business, the IRS thanks you for your success. My dad (an enrolled agent with the IRS) always says that if you pay taxes, that means you made money. No tax rate is 100%, and it's not even 50%, so you get to keep most of it. It would be nice to keep all of it, but we don't live in that world. We get to share. Be happy that you have something to share, even if you don't like how that share is spent.

In the fatalist words of the worst meme you hear, "It is what it is."

Taxes

With the new tax law in the U.S. and the complexities of international taxes, no person's situation is identical to anyone else's.

The best thing I can tell you is to keep great records. You should (keyword is *should* because we have been able to in the past) be able to deduct your expenses as an author without having to go the depreciation route. For example, a farmer buys a tractor which retains value over a number of years so the farmer cannot deduct the full cost of the tractor in the purchase year.

I deduct my travel because I write every day, no matter where I am. I also put scenes from those places into my books. It's research. It's a writing retreat. I deduct the airline ticket, taxi, rental car, hotel, and use a per diem for my meals. I also deduct any conference fees, which is one of the reasons I travel.

At home, I do not take a home office deduction. I don't want to lose the tax deduction should we sell our home or get a visit from any federal agency to verify that my office is up to code. It is, but I refuse to allow a warrantless search of my home. That's a lawyer thing for me. I deduct two phones and a mifi that I bought for the business. I get a bill that is nice and clean and stuff it into a file each and every month. I also deduct any software that I buy like Grammarly and any membership fees, like $100 a year for NINC (Novelists Inc). When I get a new computer or add-on, I deduct that because I use my computer for work. Work is all I do. I don't have any games loaded or anything like that.

I pay people, so I deduct the costs for my editor, my assistant, and joint royalties from collaborations or anthologies. Let me talk about the 1099-MISC. We are supposed to issue one of those to anyone to whom we've paid more than $600. Unless it's royalties, and then the threshold is only $10 (https://www.irs.gov/instructions/i1099msc). But wait, if you pay through an electronic service like PayPal or with a credit card, you don't have to issue a 1099-MISC as there's a record.

But there is a huge gray area. PayPal doesn't issue a 1099-K, which is a report of transfers that they share with the IRS, unless the individual has received over $20,000 AND has made over 200 transactions. Somewhere between $10 and $20,000 is what you've sent and you want to deduct it. My father is an enrolled agent with the IRS and he said that people only get in trouble if they don't issue a 1099 when they should, not if they send one when they don't have to.

So, if you pay royalties by paper check to anyone (and I have because of some old-school authors), then you need to send those individuals a 1099-MISC.

I also send one to my assistant and my editor as they are both working for me as sub-contractors. There is no duplicate reporting. PayPal's 1099-K doesn't take the place of a 1099-MISC. The person won't be double-taxed. Once is quite enough. I have an accountant who generates these for me along with the 1096, which is the form that you have to send to the IRS to inform them that you've issued 1099-MISCs. How do you get the information you need to fill out a 1099-MISC? Why, that's from a form W-9. Keep them on file, but keep them secure, as you'll have the person's social security number and you can get in a lot of trouble for releasing any of that information to the public.

And none of that applies to non-US Citizens who live and work outside the United States. Be free! And don't forget to pay your taxes to your home country.

What else do I deduct? Advertising. I deduct a lot of advertising. Keep good records. Some people use software like "Wave" that interfaces with your bank account to detail your costs. I use a spreadsheet and a lot of folders because I print everything. If I get audited, I have a mountain of paperwork that I will bring with me, all sorted into its own folders and spreadsheets that I have backed up, just in case. Redundant records are happy records.

I buy some of my own paperbacks to have on hand and use as giveaways. This is product and the key is to make sure that you don't have any on hand come the new year, otherwise you get to pay taxes on it as if you sold it at full retail.

I buy a lot of gifts for people who help me. I deduct them under a client recognition category. I buy dinners for people. Get the receipt and list everyone who was present. Last year's rules allowed a 50% deduction for those costs. It's worth it.

Copyright & Keeping Your Books Safe

The term of copyright for a particular work depends on several factors, including whether it has been published, and, if so, the date of first publication. As a general rule, for works created after January 1, 1978, copyright protection lasts for the life of the author plus an additional 70 years. For an anonymous work, a pseudonymous work, or a work made for hire, the copyright endures for a term of 95 years from the year of its first publication or a term of 120 years from the year of its creation, whichever expires first. For works first published prior to 1978, the term will vary depending on several factors. To determine the length of copyright protection for a particular work, consult chapter 3 of the Copyright Act (title 17 of the United States Code).

Unscrupulous souls will download your book and steal it. It is a fact of life. Most sites that offer "free" books that have been illegally obtained are filled with malware and viruses. But some come across as legitimate. Hands down, the best service to use is Blasty. (https://blasty.co/). You register your books and they issue the takedown notices. Easy as pie. The free version is more time-consuming, but it'll save you a lot of grief and worry. Blasty will issue the takedown notices for you so whenever anyone does an honest Google search for your books, they'll only find your legitimate outlets.

The following is straight from the U.S. Patent and Trademark Office:
How can I secure a copyright?

This is a frequently misunderstood topic because many people believe that you must register your work before you can claim copyright. However, no publication, registration or other action in the Copyright Office is required to secure copyright. Copyright is secured automatically when the work is created, and a work is "created" when it is fixed in a "copy or a phonorecord for the first time." For example, a song can be fixed in sheet music or on a CD, or both. Although registration with the Copyright Office is not required to secure protection, it is highly recommended for the following reasons:

- Registration establishes a public record of the copyright claim.
- Registration is necessary before an infringement suit may be filed in court (for works of U. S. origin).
- If made before or within 5 years of publication, registration establishes prima facie evidence in court of the validity of the copyright and of the facts stated in the certificate.
- If registration is made within 3 months after publication of the work or prior to an infringement of the work, statutory damages and attorney's fees will be available to the copyright owner in court actions. Otherwise, only an

award of actual damages and profits is available to the copyright owner.
- Registration allows the owner of the copyright to record the registration with the U. S. Customs Service for protection against the importation of infringing copies.

FOUR

PUBLISHING ON AMAZON

- Launch Checklist
- Cover Art
- Title
- Keywords
- Blurb
- Categories
- Age & Grade
- Digital Rights Management
- Upload your eBook
- Other Upload Issues
- Launch Pricing
- Resources for going wide (on all platforms versus Amazon exclusive)
- Release Schedule
- Serials and an 18-Day Release Schedule

Launch Checklist

To prepare for launch, I put together my upload blurb, keywords, description, and category file while I'm writing the book so come upload time, there is no fumbling or checking back to make sure the series title is exactly the same—critical so Amazon can link your books on a series page, which they'll do automatically if you have your words identical.

Here's what I used for Scott Moon and my Darklanding series book 1. We adjust the keywords every now and then, but these were what we used for the initial roll out.

Title: *Assignment Darklanding*
Subtitle:
Series: *Darklanding Book 01*

Description:

A frontier world. One Sheriff. And all the action one Spaceport can't hold. Darklanding is the wild west of known space. Sheriff Thaddeus Fry will never completely leave the battlefields of Centauri Prime. His new assignment, the sheriff's office of Darklanding, could be a do-nothing job, or if he's like the former sheriff, do something that could get him killed.

The Company Man, is not who he expected, to say the least. His new accommodations are right in the center of Darklanding's misfits. He finds one native of Ungwilook willing to talk to him and tries to make him a deputy. But what really matters on Darklanding, are the mines.

Faced with a dangerous collapse that could kill hundreds of workers, he leaps into action and gets the story of Darklanding started. Fans of Firefly, Bonanza, and Tombstone will love this new series. Join us today and every 18 days, you'll get a new episode of Darklanding.

Categories:
  Science Fiction > Space Adventure
  Science Fiction > Dystopian

. . .

Keywords:

Space Western frontier colonization
Space Frontier Alien Contact
Space Opera SciFi evil company overlords
Science Fiction colonial adventure
Classic Western Sheriff saloon
Galactic Empire Colonization
Wild west episode serials

One liners ad copy:

A Space Sheriff, Aliens, and The Company – who's the good guy?

The Sagittarian conglomerate made him the sheriff, and now he has to make it right.

When a war veteran becomes the sheriff on a backwater planet, justice is a one-man show.

Firefly meets Tombstone in this exciting new space opera serial.

A Space Sheriff, Aliens, The Company – and all the trouble one spaceport can't handle.

When a war veteran becomes the sheriff on a backwater planet, justice is a one-man show. Firefly meets Tombstone in the first of this new 12-episode serial, a new episode published every 18 days.

A Space Sheriff, Aliens, The Company – and all the trouble one spaceport can't handle.

Here is my publication checklist, for reference. Keep in mind that I am exclusive to Amazon. If you are wide, then this applies for your Amazon part and then going through D2D or a similar service will be helpful. If you upload direct to the major distributors (Apple, Kobo, Barnes & Noble), then you'll need a separate checklist for each of those and that's what makes D2D such an attractive option as each retailer has their own learning curve.

Publication Checklist

Action	Completed
Before Creating EBook Files	
Complete MSS, including editing.	☐
Acquire cover in highest res at 5:8 ratio, at least 1500x2400	☐
Create Front Matter and Back Matter	☐
Update ARC instruction document, if using one	☐
Build SmartURL for ARC Distribution, if desired	☐
Build SmartURL for Amazon purchase link	☐
Build SmartURL for review link in eBook	☐
Alert Social Media about upcoming book	☐

Before creating KDP Draft Entry:

Down-sample the cover to 640 wide and 320 wide versions, for NLs ☐

Solicit ARC readers, if desired ☐

Research blurb ☐

Research categories (total of ten) ☐

Research keywords ☐

Build book file using your favorite program (Word, Adobe, Scrivener, Jutoh) ☐

Build BookFunnel entry for ARC, load book file into BookFunnel ☐

Send out NL about upcoming book ☐

Send out ARC emails, if desired ☐

Update blog/website with news ☐

Back up ALL Files, preferably on permanent media like CD/DVD ☐

Create KDP Draft Entry
Complete all fields in KDP entry ☐

Load Blurb ☐

Select two 'best fit' categories ☐

Load Keywords ☐

Load Bookfile ☐

Load Cover ☐

Have price ready (all countries) ☐

Hit Publish ☐

After hitting publish:
Wait for ASIN to post on Amazon ☐

Update spreadsheet & data collection tools (add ASIN & book in series) ☐

Update all SmartURL links (purchase and review links) ☐

Get FB posts ready (with link preloaded) ☐

Update affiliate links for website (Amazon's Affiliate Program) ☐

When Amazon shows book live:
Launch FB posts ☐

Add to Author Central page ☐

Send email to Amazon to add other eight categories ☐

Get Affiliate link ☐

Update webpage ☐

Update SmartURL with links to book for major markets ☐

Update Blog ☐

Send Newsletter ☐

Update others for Author NL Swaps, including full and low res images ☐

Check in on Goodreads to see if the new book posted ☐

- [ ] Check in on Goodreads to see if the new book posted

- [ ] Update the eBook file with a link to do a Review right after "The End"

- [ ] Once the book file can be updated - reupload with review link

GET BACK TO WRITING THE NEXT BOOK

You'll notice that I don't have "Check book ranking and also-boughts by compulsively clicking refresh" or any of the other ego boosters. Understand, I do it, too, but a lot less than I used to.

I do a lot of online promotion on launch day, responding to fan comments about the launch and especially praising those who are first to review or even just the first to read the book and leave a comment on Facebook.

I know many authors don't follow Goodreads, but Amazon bought Goodreads because that's where the readers hang out. You might see something interesting. That's why I check. It's also nice to see the number of readers who have the book in their TBR (to be read) pile or listed it as currently reading.

Booklaunch.com has a great checklist that is worth checking out to give you a different and more extensive view of tracking what you need to do and when you need to do it.

Cover Art

I will always recommend getting the best cover you can for your book. That doesn't mean getting the most expensive one. Some of my less expensive covers are great. What makes a great cover?

1. Needs to speak to the genre (you do this by looking at the top 100 covers for that genre – what stands out consistently?)
2. Needs to be visible and understandable at thumbnail size (many readers will buy directly from their phones – make sure they can see your main cover details at the smallest resolution)
3. Brand consistency – set your brand to make sure that readers can subconsciously link your books
4. Coloring is important but contrast will give you the low-res legibility you need

I am not a visual arts kind of person, but I know a lot of people who are. I hire graphic designers to do covers, because the best artwork does not necessarily make for the best cover. You have to have great art and a great cover. Artists don't necessarily make for the best typographers. I've had three people work on my covers, a photographer/photoshop expert, a graphic designer/illustrator, and a typographer. Here's the end result.

In the next example below, here is an expensive cover that is great artwork, but had to be lightened for the final presentation. If you step back, you'll see that the image fades away.

So we went with some different

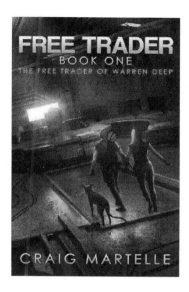

typography, a little lightening, and came up with the following.

There are no hard and fast rules with covers, so all anyone can ever give you is an opinion and the opinions that matter most are the readers of your genre. If you check online, you'll find that most of the covers that get awards are literary fiction in style, which should tell you that those awards are like a self-licking ice cream cone. What's the purpose?

To sell more books! That's always the purpose. So use the cover that will sell more books, and that means listening to the readers. After you've put out a book or two, canvass your readers. Send out a poll in your newsletter asking basic questions: how did you find my books; what did you like about them; does this cover grab you, etc. You'll also find your superfans that way. Send one or two respondents to your poll a signed paperback or something personal.

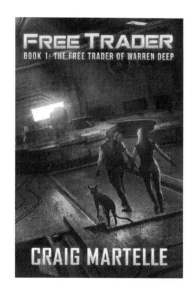

At Christmas, one-year Kindle Unlimited subscriptions were discounted to $80. I gave a bunch of those away to my fans through various contests, plus I gave all my beta readers a subscription. (Even though they had KU already, it extended their renewal date by a year.)

Title

It is important to get your title right. When you come up with something, ask people what they think the book will be about. My Free Trader series is going to get re-titled at some point. Free Trader of Warren Deep. Seriously?

Yes, that's my title for a space adventure. But trade is key! I argue. That's fine, but don't put it into the title! I have six books, soon to be nine books, strapped to this name. I have to work extra hard to get people to look beyond the title to see the space adventure within. A better title would have been "A Young Man and his Mindlinked Cat" or even "A New World Among the Stars."

Live and learn, but nothing is a show-stopper. It was just harder. Work smarter, not harder like I did.

For titles, shorter is better. Action or suspense is good. I love Jennifer Foehner-Wells's title, Fluency, with the spaceship on the cover. Well done! It makes you think about how would we converse with aliens, which is exactly what the book is about.

Or Richard Fox's Iron Dragoons with a cover showing the head of a mechanized soldier. That book won the Dragon Award, because people could get into it, from cover to blurb to story. It all worked perfectly.

Keywords

These keywords are different from AMS keywords (far different). You do not get to put other author names in here. You get up to fifty characters and can put phrases or a bunch of keywords.

I've done both the stacking and individual words. By stacking, I put a number of keywords together and that gets me into the categories I want without having to email Amazon. (More on that below.) In my example above for Darklanding, I used these keywords.

Keywords:

Space Western frontier colonization
Space Frontier Alien Contact
Space Opera SciFi evil company overlords
Science Fiction colonial adventure
Classic Western Sheriff saloon
Galactic Empire Colonization

Wild west episode serials

I dutifully checked them using KDP Rocket and found that most did not have a high impact. Western by itself was good. Galactic Empire was good, as was Colonization. The jury was out about evil company overlords, but I had to leave that in for my own edification, and so on. You want keywords here that someone perusing Amazon might use so that your book shows up in their search results.

Which is the same thing you are doing with the keywords in your ads, but you can have a thousand of those. You want your books to show up to those searching and to those browsing particular categories. Keep that in mind as you select your keywords. If anyone searches Amazon for Western sheriff saloon, Darklanding will show up first.

Blurb

The blurb is an ad for your book, not a synopsis. Keep that in mind from the outset. Blurbs are considered copywriting. Look at it from the outside. What entices you as a reader when you see a blurb? A laundry list of back story? A bunch of character and place names?

How about a dilemma? I love Richard Fox's tagline for his Ember War series. "The Earth is doomed. Humanity has a chance."

One of the best in the business is Bryan Cohen, whose book *How to Write a Sizzling Synopsis* gives numerous examples to help you understand and guide you through the process. Bryan offers the following three questions:

1. What problem are you solving?

2. How is your book the solution? Or at the least, what are people getting out of your book?

3. How will this entertain or change them?

The simplest things aren't simple at all. The best blurbs are short and high-impact. They get into your head like a clever jingle and won't let go. YOU HAVE TO READ THIS BOOK! You have to read it because the dilemma speaks to you. You have to know what happens next. You've embraced the character and their challenges and want to share their lives.

Brian Meeks suggests using engaging words. (You'll find them in his book on *Mastering Amazon Ads*.) Combine them into a call to action like, "What would you do?" This is powerful phraseology because it doesn't presume success. "Will Anita save the day?" Of course she will, unless it's a dark horror book, and then her efforts at hiding in the basement among the creepy taxidermist's knife set probably won't end well. A question to make the reader think.

Here is my best converting blurb. It converts at anywhere from 1 to 4 to 1 to 8, and yes, I violate the 'can he save the world?' question that I just told you to avoid.

A Cat and his human minions fight to bring peace to humanity.

- "Craig Martelle is a masterful writer with a grand imagination."
- "Reminiscent of science fiction of the 60s. Sort of a cross between Star Man's Son 2250AD by Andre Norton and Robert Heinlein's Tunnel in the Sky."
- "You clearly are, like the great Asimov, a master of Science Fiction."

The Free Trader takes you to a world across the galaxy, where humans are not the only sentient species. After a devastating war, humanity and its creations rise again. The Free Trader finds himself at a crossroads - **can he and his Cat prevent a repeat of past mistakes?**

And the follow-on series...
Cygnus Space Opera (set in the Free Trader Universe)
Book 1 - Cygnus Rising
Book 2 - Cygnus Expanding
Book 3 - Cygnus Arrives

I included the follow-on books because those don't show up on the series page, so I keep the readers informed that not only is there soon to be nine books in the series, there's a follow-on series, too. The readership that I've developed read a great number of books, so telling them there are twelve books in the series is beneficial.

On a side note, there is some question about using quotes within the book description. It seems like it may be a violation of Amazon's TOS, but I've never heard of anyone getting their book taken down for using them. I no longer put quotes in mine, but I do have some older blurbs that I'm leaving alone and hoping that Amazon grandfathers them in under any new interpretation.

Categories

How do you know which category is best for your book? That is both an ego and a business question. Getting a bestseller tag in a lesser known category looks good and helps in visibility, I believe, but the only thing that really matters is the bottom line—the gross number of sales. (Rank is made up of sales and borrows if you are exclusive to Amazon in KDP Select.)

Visibility helps with sales. Reviews help with sales. Getting Amazon to push your book helps with sales, and there are a lot of guesstimates on how you get Amazon to do that. I haven't seen any that are definitive beyond selling more books.

Books that sell well seem to continue to sell well. Some of that could be through word of mouth or exposure in the also-boughts, which is free promotion above the sponsored ads listing. Recently, we've seen that some titles don't get the also-bought line populated. That is worrisome as the only way to show people your book on similar books is by paying for ads.

And that goes back to making sure you are in the right category for your book. KDP Rocket (a Kindlepreneur product from Dave Chesson) has a new feature called Category Hunter. This is an exceptional addition to help you research where you will find the most traction for like books. You want to get on their also-boughts so people looking for that type of book see yours—with your engaging cover that makes them click and 'read more.'

Find a combination of categories that will give you visibility in the category with the most books where you still could see a top twenty ranking. For example, I compete in the space opera category of science fiction. Today (March 14th, 2018), the book sitting at number one is selling 629 copies with an overall Amazon book rank of 174 while the 20th book in the category is selling 105 copies and has an overall Amazon book rank of 1321. That is a pretty robust category with a lot of competition. But then I can put my book into Alien Invasion as a secondary category, where the category's best-seller has an overall Amazon rank of 455 and the number 20 book in the category has an overall rank of 1438.

I know that my books will tickle the top 200, so these two categories work for me. But I could also go after the Teen & Young Adult Aliens category, which requires the books to be put in the 13 to 18+ category when uploaded. First book there is 788 overall and the 20th book is 11022. It doesn't hurt to have a bestseller tag while also being seen in popular categories with lots of visitors. A rising tide floats all boats, doesn't it?

I can't recommend KDP Rocket highly enough. If you want to make data-driven business decisions, then get the right data.

After you've selected your two categories, your book will publish. It'll show in three categories on your book's page on Amazon.com. You can add seven more categories if you want. Here's how you do that.

Updating your browse categories
Go to your Author Central Page
Click "Contact Us"
Select "My Books"
Select "Update Information About a Book"
Select "Browse Categories"
Select "I want to update my book's browse categories"
Select email and give them your book title and ASIN *(make it easy on them)*, then ask to have your book added to the additional categories, being very specific - I copy/;paste the ones I want. Like this.
• Kindle eBooks > Teen & Young Adult > Science Fiction > Action & Adventure

Show the complete category layout as I've done above. You have to make it as easy as humanly possible for the Amazon customer service agents. The easier you make it, the quicker your resolution will be.

At least that's how you might be able do it when your book goes to print. Sometimes, Amazon will email you back and tell you that they can't put the book into that category unless (there's a variety of reasons Amazon could give). If they give you an age range or keywords that have to be included, update whatever they tell you and then email them back and tell them that you've made the adjustments. The process to update your categories, if done on a weekday, could take as little as an hour. Sometimes it takes a day or two. It's important to hit these as quickly as possible while you are at the height of your sales, which for me is when I send out my newsletter on launch day.

Age & Grade

I've published a lot of books and have tried a number of different ages and age ranges. When I use 16 to 18+, Amazon puts my books in the Young Adult (YA) category. When I use 13 to 18+, same result. When I use 12 to 18+, Amazon puts my books in the Children's category.

What is the difference? When I have the F-bomb in the books or adult situations, I list them at 16 and up. No F-bomb, but some swearing (no graphic sex or anything like that), then it's 13 and up. If there is neither, then I go with 12 and up. I know what I read when I was 12 (Robert E. Howard's Conan the Barbarian series), and that's what I use as the gauge.

I never touch grade. I expect that is for books that market to specific grades, like books intended to be used in a classroom.

Digital Rights Management

This is a one-way trip. If you take it, then legitimate buyers could have trouble with downloading your book. It is supposedly an anti-piracy measure, but it doesn't work. Pirates will have a pdf copy of your book on launch day without issue. I never select DRM anymore.

Upload your eBook Manuscript

This is a simple process. Many people use Vellum. I upload directly using my Word file. This is right from the Amazon upload page—recommended formats for Kindle eBooks: .doc, .docx, HTML, MOBI, ePub, RTF, Plain Text, and KPF.

Amazon's format is MOBI. If that's what you format in, then your conversion should look exactly like what you see on your screen. For me, it changes a little from my Word file when Amazon converts it, but they make it look great. If you have a bunch of sexy fonts within your story, they may get neutered. Amazon creates a single standard where the users can select which font and at which size they can read their eBook. Save your sexy fonts for the paperback version where you have a much greater level of visual control.

Other Upload Issues

Make sure you address the spelling errors that come up. There will always be some. If the spelling is what you want, then click "Ignore" and Amazon will okay your book. This will also keep you from getting an automated quality alert. Amazon's system has caught typos for me. I back out, correct them, and re-upload the manuscript. It's okay to take your time at this point. Don't hurry an error into production.

Launch Pricing

- Full price
- Discount for 1 day
- Discount for a week or so
- Amazon Giveaway (buy at 99 cents)

There are all kinds of schools of thought regarding pricing.

A low price can attract more buyers, reward followers, and drive your launch day rank higher. Many authors launch at full price. Hardcore fans will buy it regardless.

What is the appearance of value? This is where I'm not going to answer this question for you. As an admin on the 20Booksto50k

Facebook group, I've seen a wide variety of pricing schemes. What you have to keep in mind are the following:

- Genre—what is the average in your genre?
- Your experience—known authors can command higher prices.
- Book length—selling a 300k word book for the same as a 30k word book doesn't make much sense.
- Value proposition—how do the readers perceive the value? And in the end, they are the only voices that matter.

I started off pricing all my books at $2.99. This allowed me to discount books to 99 cents and run paid promotions like Ereader News Today, Robin Reads, Book Barbarian, and more. (There's a big number of paid newsletter promotion services.)

Some genres rate eBook prices of $9.99. Under-served audiences who are hungry for more material—Pride and Prejudice novels are some of those in this category and those who write well in that category command high prices and make a great living.

Other categories seem set at $3.99. When I look at the top 20 books in a category, I'll look at reviews and prices to gauge how long a particular book will stay there. If a book is showing at $4.99 in the number two spot and has 300 reviews, the book for 99 cents in the number one spot with four reviews won't be there for long. The low price drove sales up and got the rank. When the price changes back, will new readers still find it attractive? That's a marketing and conversion question that we'll talk about later.

In the Terry Henry Walton Chronicles, the first books were about 60k words and we priced all of them at $3.99. By books eight, nine, and ten, I had way too many threads to tie up, so those books averaged nearly 95k words. We charged $4.99 and some readers complained, accusing us of price gouging. We even put the statement in one blurb, "Two books for the price of one!" Consistency is important and that's part of training your readership.

We tried this with our Darklanding series, books of 20k to 30k words published every eighteen days. The first book we priced at a consistent 99 cents. The others were $2.99 and that's all there was to it. We had a couple complaints in the beginning, but those died down. With each new release, we got a nice bump to the previous volumes, both in page reads and buys. Nothing sells the last book like the next book.

I saw this exemplified when I published Book 7 in my Free Trader Series, a year and a half after Book 6 hit the market. In the two weeks after Book 7 hit, I averaged ten copies a day each of the other six books. That's my blue collar approach, a solid base across a wide front and it all adds up. Before you know it, you're making $1000/day without any breakout bestsellers.

I didn't change the pricing on any of the earlier Free Trader books. Those copies sold at full price for a long stretch and as of this writing, they continue to sell at that rate, and I am doing no advertising on this series besides a minimal number of basic AMS ads and reiterating that Free Trader is alive and well in my newsletter.

I've seen people put together general guides on pricing, but I won't do that. Look at your genre and how the top books are priced. If you're not as well-known, maybe knock off a buck and go for it. I'm up to $4.99 for my mainline series, and I don't see the dropoff in sales one might expect.

Resource for Going Wide
Direct Options for eBooks:
* Amazon KDP
* Nook Press
* iTunes Producer & iTunes Connect (for iBooks)
* Kobo Writing Life
* Google Play (even though they've allegedly been closed to new authors for well over a year now with no sign of changing)

eBooks - Aggregators

* Draft2Digital
* StreetLib
* Smashwords

Print

* Amazon CreateSpace
* KDP Print (Beta)
* IngramSpark
* Lulu
* Blurb
* Off-set printing

Release Schedule

Only you can determine when you are ready to release your book. You can do a pre-order or you can simply release it when ready. A pre-order adds a level of stress and complication that I don't need so I don't do them unless I have the final book ready but am waiting to release for some reason, like a heavily promoted launch.

If you miss your pre-order date, Amazon will cancel your pre-order privileges for one year. Sometimes, you update the file before the four-day cutoff window closes, but Amazon still sends out the wrong file. What do you do? You contact them and hope for the best.

No one fully knows how Amazon's algorithms work, but everyone says that you want to be on their good side.

Whatever that means. Amazon is a commercial retailer. They make money when you sell books. They'll give your stuff a little push if it looks like people are buying. That's about the extent of my understanding of how it works. There is so much that goes into putting a book in front of a potential buyer, no one source is the end-all. I stay on the good side by releasing quickly and promoting within Amazon itself through AMS ads.

Another way to get exposure is by getting into the also-boughts, that listing immediately below the top part of the product page where Amazon suggests books based on what others buy after buying your book. In order to populate the also-boughts and get on other people's front page for extra exposure and hopefully sales, you need to sell at least fifty copies.

You might have an ad with catchy language today, but it isn't catchy tomorrow. You never know what will trigger jumps, but when sales are good, they seem to remain good. More of that and less of the bad sales!

Help Amazon to help you by releasing regularly. If you release less often than once per month, which is most people, one of the better ways to improve your situation is spreading out your sales over a few days. Get your bump with your main list, but get help with NL swaps and run ads. Market to your target audience, even if it is only a boosted post off your FB author page.

Rapid release is all about exploiting the algorithm. The best numbers I saw were from the first series getting released exactly seven days apart. This presumes that you get sales on the first book. You'll get no love from Amazon if you aren't moving any product. Remember that they are a retailer and don't care who you are or that you're a person who just put her baby up for sale. Did you sell it? No? Well then, Amazon won't like you as much as the person who is moving all kinds of product.

You can make your own luck by selling books. How do we do that? That's the million-dollar question, but it all starts with one book at a time. When you figure out how that one book sold, you can work that magic on a second and a third. Keep at it.

What about a less rapid release?

Serials and an 18-Day Release Schedule

Scott Moon and I undertook writing a space western in TV serial style. Our target was 30k words per book. I wrote the first book and it was only 17k words, but we are keeping it priced at $0.99, with all the rest priced at $2.99. Scott wrote most of the rest. (I wrote Books 6 and 9.) Book 2 was 23k words, and Books 3-5 and beyond were in the vicinity of 30k words. We started last September to build our kitty of readily available titles so there would be no hiccup in meeting our 18-day launch windows.

Our costs per title are $200, which includes cover and editing. My FB and AMS ad spend is about $2/day total.

We launched Book 1 on December 18th, with some NL swaps and a little AMS ad love, but low spend. We launched Book 2 on Jan 5, and Book 3 on Jan 23. (Part of our tagline is a new release every 18 days.) On Jan 23, we ran Book 1 for free.

Look at how the tail is increasing in size for both sales and page reads. This is a Space Western (*Firefly* meets *Tombstone*, although we put it in the space opera and alien contact categories). It's not a huge niche with a ready market, so we are developing that market. Many reviews call Book 1 a Short Story, and that's part of the message that we didn't manage. We call them all "books," which has no defined word count, and the average reader doesn't know what a novella is. The reviews are overwhelmingly positive, but length is part of the readers' concern, so we'll start managing that part in FB ads—so much story in a compact, quick-read package kind of thing.

There was a little hiccup going from 1 to 2 as the price also went from 99 cents to $2.99, even though subsequent volumes were longer. We did not attempt to work this message because it will play out over time, when we can tout 'Book 1 in the bestselling Darklanding series is ONLY 99 cents' for marketing).

Overall, this is a win as it is starting to sustain itself. Six weeks after launch, Book 1 continues to get 10-15 sales a day and over 1000 page reads. Are these numbers eye-popping? No, but we are having a lot of fun and the income is increasing with each new title. We also wanted a series that was pitchable to network TV, because, hey! Those bastards canceled *Firefly* and still haven't replaced it with something comparable...

FIVE

BUILDING A FOLLOWING

- Biggest Bang for the Buck
- Snippets, Blogs, and Social Media – Oh my!
- How do you build a following?
- Newsletter Cross Promotion
- New Release Notification
- Getting Feedback
- Trolls

Biggest bang for the buck or how can I get the most exposure at the least cost?

I get 100 emails and 50 direct messages a day from people. Maybe I can answer some of those questions here. New authors who have yet to publish universally struggle with this question. Here are some tips and a not-all-inclusive list of things. Some established authors are looking to start fresh. It all applies. I've said some of this before, but here's a recap with value estimate.

- Social media: you have it anyway, use it to build your author brand. Be interesting and be well-spoken. Be

professional. This costs nothing but time. If your posts are laced with typos and incomprehensible, you won't be taken seriously as an author. Well-written posts could gain you readers. Poorly written posts will not.
- Read books in the genre you are/will be writing in. Don't write in a genre you know nothing about. That is a steep mountain and high, too.
- Get a thick skin. When you're new, it is easy to get discouraged. Remember why you write—because you love it.
- The first 500 words of your story have to be killer. The reader has to be wowed and be fanatical about wanting to read more. If you need back story for the rest of your story to make sense and your back story is boring, you will have to work it in without an info dump to start your story. You don't want to fight through that to develop a following. You want the readers to follow because they're interested, not because they've been badgered.
- Help promote other authors by finding stuff you like in your genre. This can build your genre-specific following by identifying those folks who might read your stuff. You can boost a FB post every now and then with a similar style book for $10 or $20. See the readers who are clicking that. Then you can ask if they'd like a free story and you can send yours. See if you can start building your readership.
- Your book needs to be edited. Editing can be done by beta readers if you can find them or by software such as Grammarly—which is inexpensive, and good, but not an end-all. Self-edited books usually look it. (No offense to those who can pull it off, but usually, you are already well-established and know what you're doing.)
- Covers: research the covers in your genre and then look through the pre-made cover providers and see if

something is as close as you can get to your book. These will cost $100 to $200 or so. If you can do it yourself, understand good cover design and not necessarily great art. They are not one and the same.
- Reserve your domain name and if you can afford it, start building a website. You need a real email. (If you show up with an AOL email, people won't take you seriously, and AOL emails sometimes get blocked by other email providers as AOL has been compromised too many times.)
- Publish: It costs nothing to publish on Amazon and then you can use AMS ads, which are relatively low cost.

Total cost to publish? $250 and a bunch of time. Total cost to be taken seriously as an author? There is no price on that because that comes from the stuff you can't buy—a great story, well-written, a public persona that readership in your genre can relate to and want to follow, and a work ethic that says, I can do this.

Snippets, Blogs, and Social Media – Oh my!

Snippets are bits and pieces of your story. You can post them on your blog or directly to Facebook, maybe even 140 characters at a time on Twitter. Some people have success on Instagram, but the base premise is the same. Share bits and pieces of the story to build interest without the hard sell.

The Hillcat looked up, disdain clear on his furry face.

"Why are you such an ass?" the human asked. The cat yawned, found the human's blanket, and curled up.

I could post that with a picture of the cat and a coming soon, Snippet #2 from The Free Trader... Yes, I have a series with a cat as a main character, and don't be surprised at the demographics of my readership.

I've posted entire chapters before as part of a cover reveal. I always share the cover well before the book goes live. I believe the cover drives excitement. I always share my ever-growing cover wall because I am proud of my covers. I've had quite a few re-done. That's okay. It drives up the cost per book, but always pays off. I have never had a new cover not pay for itself, even on my short stories.

The whole thing is to generate interest. Write well and share it. I can put more on my blog and that gives me more flexibility with formatting (something as simple as italics) and then link to the blog from one of my Facebook pages.

Have a great visual to accompany your snippet—your cover or even other artwork. I've downloaded graphics from DepositPhoto at a total bargain price and used those to generate interest in my books on my social media because I could relate a scene to what was shown in the picture that I bought for one dollar. The license allowed for that. (Always make sure what the license on these photos allows. If it says private use only, don't get it!)

If you are exclusive to Amazon, you cannot give away more than 10% of your book. If your story is 60k words, you can post up to 6k worth of snippets. That's a lot of snippets. Or you can post all 60k, but take down those posts the second you hit publish. The limitation is that you can't give away more than 10% while you are exclusive. Before you publish, you can do whatever you want. It's your book and the only person you need to answer to is yourself. It's nice being the boss, so take good care of your best employee.

How do you build a following?

I addressed this in Chapter 2, but not in detail. I am personally a fan of building a following organically—those people who like your writing. Secondarily, I like people who like my genre. I am not a fan of people who will sign up for my newsletter because I'm giving away an Amazon gift card. I know a lot of authors who do this, counting on the numbers game. Ten percent of 100,000 people is still 10,000 good folks, but what if it's one percent or less? My experience with pure freebie promotions that are unrelated to my books in any way, not genre and not me as an author, is that it is a fraction of a percent who are engaged. I pay to maintain an email subscriber list. A fraction of a percent does not cover my costs in maintaining the extra number of names. So I don't do these anymore. I do targeted list-building efforts only.

InstaFreebie and BookFunnel can fill the void in providing a forum where you upload your reader sample—up to a full book if you want. Both sites will collect email addresses of those who want to download your offering. You don't have to have a mandatory opt-in, but I always use it. That is my minimum price to get my stuff for free. I offer one of my short stories that I also have on Amazon for 99 cents —it's not in Kindle Select (KU), so I can offer it elsewhere. If a reader doesn't want to give me their email, they can still get the story and I'll get their 35 cents. That is a reasonable trade, for me.

I only use BookFunnel, because it does everything I need it to do. I bought the big package from them so I can do whatever I need to do however many times I need to do it. I don't use it anywhere near what I need to in order to get my money's worth, but it is there. I've run some group promotions off my BookFunnel because I can support 5000 downloads.

That's neither here nor there, but it is a good segue into another methodology for gaining quality followers.

A cross promotion.

The single best effort to add quality subscribers to my list came through a ten-author anthology. We each wrote space opera, so we all had a lot in common. We provided a short story that I consolidated under a nice cover. We formatted it and made it available via BookFunnel. We each notified our own email lists. And then I ran narrowly targeted ads on Facebook as well, looking only at space opera fans who also were Kindle readers.

We picked up 1400 new subscribers that we shared among the

ten of us. (We had that disclaimer in numerous places throughout the anthology—signing up to get the book signed the person up for ten lists.) I have lost about 400 of those, but the remaining 1000 are the highest quality—readers willing to pay for good space opera stories. Many have become superfans and those folks are worth their weight in gold. The total cost for 1400 email addresses? It would have been zero had I not run the FB ads, but as it turned out, it was about $40 total.

And that's why you don't run Facebook ads to collect email subscribers. Those cost $1 to $2 each to get. That is probably the most expensive thing you can do to find subscribers. I paid a couple hundred dollars for less than that many new subscribers and the worst part is, I'm not sure they are all that great. If I had a one for one buy-rate, then I would get an ROI at that cost. But I don't. So I don't gather names that way.

The great thing about most email services is that you can parse the names of the signups. Use a separate link and list for those who sign up from your back matter. The back matter is what you put at the end of your book. If someone finished reading your story and continued into the back matter, then you have a winner. And if they then clicked on the link to join your newsletter list from there (or typed it in), then you have a fan and the making of a superfan. Keep those people segregated. You can carry on conversations with them, get feedback, give them samples of your work while you're writing, and they become your superstar beta team. If you get too many fans signing up via your backmatter... That's a ridiculous statement. You can never have too many superfans. Nurture them and they will be your foundation to a hugely successful career.

Newsletter Cross Promotion

"Hey, Bob! You write space opera. I write space opera. How about a swap? I'll promote your next release when it comes out and you promote mine."

That is the crux of a swap. It can work out well and is generally between peers, those authors on the same plateau on the climb up the mountain of success, which is best left to the readership to determine. The attitude that makes this work is that a rising tide lifts all boats. Readers can read far more than we can write. Sharing a group and opening your readers' eyes to a bigger world is a great thing. The readers will determine what they like and what they don't like. It also helps you raise your game. If you are swapping with authors that you think write better than you, what are you going to do about it? Me? I'd pay my editor a bonus to crank up the heat!

Having a list of 30,000 names doesn't mean you're a successful author, it only means that you have a lot of email addresses. Are they buyers? I would much rather share with a smaller list with a higher engagement rate than a list of 100,000 subscribers who don't care and funnel the note directly to their spam folder, if they are real people, that is.

But be careful. If you promote someone to your fans, you need to make sure that their book will satisfy your fans. At least skim the book in question, unless you know the author and their work. Remember when we talked about brand? Everything you do once you hit publish goes to your brand. You promote poorly written books with bad covers, then you will not be doing yourself any favors. You don't have to crush a budding author, but you can tell them, "I have certain expectations from my readers and this book won't fit with what they like."

New Release Notification

The bread and butter of publishing. This is your first impression of the readers' first impression of your book. Are they buying it? Do they remember that you exist? And that's why you have a newsletter, so you don't have to work so hard at providing content on a blog where they stop by every day to see what's new.

On publication day, you send your newsletter. Did you send one before publication day to let them know it was coming? Did you do any snippets? Did you whet the appetite by sharing artwork? Hungry readers are one-click buyers. Set them up and they will reward you.

Amazon will send an email to everyone who follows you. So how do you get Amazon followers?

Organically, because they clicked 'follow' when they were looking at your books on Amazon. You can also run giveaways and in this case, numbers are king, because you pay nothing to maintain the list. I gave a Kindle Paperwhite. I ran a bunch of Facebook ads, but also clicked for Amazon to open it up to anyone looking. The only condition to enter to win? Follow me on Amazon. I've run hundreds of giveaways using my books as well as other books from authors in my genre (with their permission, of course, although you can give anything away on Amazon—scroll to the bottom of the product page until you see the Giveaway button).

By my count, I could have as few as a thousand followers on Amazon or as many as ten thousand. Amazon does not share that information, but I do pick up a number of sales when they send out their notifications. I follow myself, so yes, I get my own notifications.

BookBub is the gold standard when it comes to maintaining a parsed email subscriber list. Set up your BookBub author page and make sure you add your books every time you have a new release. If it fits in their criteria, they'll send out an alert to your followers. This alert looks just like a Featured Deal, so take advantage, because this doesn't cost you anything. Create your author profile at the partners.-bookbub.com site and go to town.

- Claimed in your author profile within seven days of publication
- Novels and Novellas: 70+ pages
- Nonfiction: 100+ pages
- Cookbooks: 70+ pages
- Children's picture books: 20+ pages

There are some paid newsletter subscribers that will do new release pitches for you, but the value of those may not be what you want. Hit your social media, release your newsletter, make your blog post, share with like-minded authors, and promote the book with real ads.

Yes, ads. You are a small business so you get to do all the things, but they aren't overwhelming. I am very light on ads, myself, so I count on the professionals to guide me through their works on the subjects.

Facebook Ads? Buy Michael Cooper's book, *Help! My Facebook Ads Suck*. He's also responsive if you have questions. He's just a downright good guy who like numbers and data-crunching. He also writes great books so his stuff sells when marketed correctly. He shares all of that in his book.

Amazon Marketing Services (AMS) Ads? Buy Brian Meeks' book, *Mastering Amazon Ads*. Brian has a Facebook group for people to share results and tweak their approach. It takes work, but damn! You can make some money...assuming you have some great books and listen closely to the advice, incrementally putting it into practice.

Getting Feedback

Getting feedback on your books is like going to the doctor. You can accept one opinion and be happy, or you can get a bunch of opinions and select the one you like best. But you're still at the doctor because you have a problem. The remedy may be unpalatable or the one you like might not cure your problem.

Welcome to being your own boss. You get to decide what to do.

You, as the author, may not like the feedback you get. You may have found readers who are not in your genre OR there may be a real problem with your story.

Anyone who takes the time to tell you something deserves to be listened to. Listen for the real meaning behind what they say. Sure, some people are mean and some people have no tact, but what you hear can make the difference between your success and your failure. A romance reader may not like your alien science fiction, but she's your friend and read the book as a favor, for example.

When you first start, you lean on your friends and family. As you progress, you find that they may not be the best at giving you feedback on your book. Understand that it takes time, but if you are in a readers group and become a writer, you will be able to find people within your genre. Don't join that group specifically to thrust your book upon them. Read what they are reading and offer good feedback, without being too critical. Don't try to prove anything. As I've said before, don't be a dick. I may not like 50 *Shades of Gray*, but I can't knock a book that sold ninety million copies. It appealed to the right readers at the right time. Good for E.L. James. And that is as critical as I would get in a group of readers or authors.

How can you make sure you accept the right feedback and then take the best action for your business?

Split Personality Disorder.

You must step away from being the artist and step into the shoes of the business owner. Looking dispassionately at your work and then analyzing what you've done to get it in front of the readers the story is most likely to appeal to. Why is or isn't it working? You need to be able to answer in either case.

I bet there is someone who knows. The readers. Ask them. There will be some who like it. There will be those who don't. If they start with, "I don't usually read Rhinoceros Horror..." then that's not who you want feedback from, although they can tell you about the quality of writing. "It flowed well, but I couldn't get into the story..."

Find the rhino lovers out there and see what they think! Even if you have to give the book away after not getting any sales. This is what a business person would do—a free sample and then have the person taking the sample fill out a survey for a coupon. It works. Start a conversation with readers in your genre and you will get better with each new word.

Look at how much and what you have to explain, because if you have to explain something to a reader, they missed it. I look at input like that as I need to write it better where they can't miss it if it is a key detail. Sometimes you do need to spoon-feed your readers. If they need to know the quadratic equation to solve a hint within your story, you may lose some readers, unless you're writing a high school textbook, and then it could be spot on. Write for the audience and write for yourself. When you find where those two things intersect, then you will be a much happier author.

Avoid the people who are too controlling. As I will always say, there are no set must-dos in this business besides one thing and that is find readers willing to pay for your work. Without that, it's not a business.

Everything else you do goes to that end. (Ethically, of course. The book stuffers and the scammers? Screw those people.)

If you can't look at your business because all you want to do is write? I don't know what to tell you besides reiterating that you're an indie. That means you do all the things. Sure, you could get an agent and try to get a traditional publisher deal, but the end result is simple. If you sign with them and make $100k in sales, you'll probably see about $10k for you. Very few authors make $100k in sales with traditional publishing. Very few.

With $10k? You'll be at your day job. With $100k in sales as an indie exclusive to Amazon? About $70k. That means you can look at your day job and not be so quagmired in the daily grind. Also, do you have enough money to pay someone else $60k so you can pocket $10k? I don't have enough money for that nor the desire, because I'm an indie and I can do all the things.

Trolls

The worst thing about being successful is the trolls, those bottom feeders who target an author so they can spew their bile in the form of one-star reviews, douchebag Facebook comments, random messages, and sometimes emails with helpful hints that aren't hints at all, but demeaning and wasteful.

First and foremost, understand that the issue is them and not you. Unfortunately, as an author, you have to maintain a certain public profile which makes you a target for trolls. So they become your issue.

Don't feed the troll! That's like responding to a one-star review on Amazon, something you just can't do. If you tried to carry on a conversation while you still thought the troll was a normal human being and they go off, cut the cord immediately.

Block them on social media. Tell your email to route their emails directly to the trash bin. Hopefully they don't have your phone number or real address.

Safety tip: get a PO Box.

Pen Names provide some level of protection, but you're still a public person as an author. The troll could haunt your pen name's persona.

Whackamole—just delete everything that comes from the troll and move on with your life. Living in fear lets them win.

When do you report them to the police or to the feds? The threshold for online criminal behavior is fairly high, unfortunately. A death threat where they also share your home address? You'll want to call the police on that one. Almost everything else is gray. If you are afraid for your safety, call the police and get advice.

Many trolls will find a new target for their ravings. You'll have to wait them out because you don't have much of a choice. If you feed them by trying to fight back, they'll hang on longer. Relegate them to anonymity and move on with your life.

What you can do is write. Keep writing and build a following of people who are happy for you, happy to read your books, and happy for your success.

SIX

WRITING THE NEXT BOOK

- Keeping Your Goals Alive
- Writing a new story (the power of a backlist)
- Improving Your Word Count
- Social Proof
- Staying Motivated (without alienating your family)
- Hitting the Wall
- The Value of Time

Keeping Your Goals Alive

The best goals are ones within your control. We all want our books to hit the top of the charts and sell zillions of copies. That might happen, but if that's your goal, you will be disappointed a great deal until you've reached that pinnacle.

What is in your control is word count, studying your craft, incorporating feedback into your continuous improvement loop, and doing better as an author with each new day. Maybe it is something as simple as helping a high schooler write and publish their first short story. You never know when the right kind word could make all the difference in someone's life.

Set your daily word count goal and then meet it and beat it until it's no longer a challenge. Then raise the bar and go again. I'm a big fan of writing every single day. It's something that I feel I have to do. It makes it so much easier to pick up in the middle of a sentence if you write every day. You'll get back into your story more quickly and the words will flow better.

When I first started writing full-time, my goal was 1000 words a day. I struggled to meet that goal for the first month. Keep in mind, I was doing it full-time and had trouble getting 1000 words. Fast forward one year. I wrote the second book in my space opera series in seventeen and a half days. It was 108,000 words in length. That's 6171 words per day.

That was my top-end. I haven't been able to do that since, although I've averaged 3500 to 4000 WPD in nearly all stories after that.

That is my sweet spot. 3500 WPD gets me a reasonable work day without too much stress and time for all the other things in a full-time author's life who also has to read a great number of stories as part of a series of anthology collections. The people submitting those stories deserve my full attention to give them the best feedback possible. My goal is 3500 WPD, for each and every day of the year.

I have different goals that involve publishing books on time, getting covers ordered months before they're needed, better managing my ad campaigns. The words are a given and my refuge.

It's the other business stuff that demands good goals.

There are standalone stories and there are series. That's it. Some books are long and some are short. Some series only have two books. Some only have short stories. (These are called serials.)

My first four books were in three different genres. I strongly recommend you don't do this, unless you are already a marketing expert and are able to parse your newsletter by genre and maintain separate lists like an old hand.

That was way more than I could handle when I first started publishing. I would recommend that you stay with one genre for at least your first few books so you can build your understanding of the processes involved in being a professional author. Changing genres means you get to do it all over again. This keeps you from building on previous gains. It steepens your learning curve, because what works in one genre may not work in another.

Marketing is easier for anything that the readers have seen before. You should already have them on the hook because of your engagement. Many wait with bated breath for the next installment, and they will always want it before it's ready. This is good stuff, because these are your hardcore fans. They'll pick up the first book in a new series because they like the way you write.

It is easier to sell ten books to one person than one book to ten different people.

Writing a new story (the power of a backlist)

I published at least one book a month for the first two and a half years that I was writing full-time, right up to the publication of this book. Add a bunch of short stories, anthologies, a few different collaborations, omnibuses, box sets, and all of a sudden, Amazon thinks I have seventy-nine titles.

I write every day and a fair number of words. I rarely delete too many words. I might move them into a different story, but dammit! I typed those words fair and square and I'm going to use them.

I love short stories because I can focus on a single topic. I get to remove the complexities of a multi-POV story and take one situation, build it three-dimensionally. Six thousand words later, I have something I can put into an anthology and get my name out there. No one knew me at the beginning. Of course. So I couldn't get into any anthologies. I started my own and everyone who wanted to come with me on the ride joined in. We threw a good cover on it and published away!

It was a great learning experience. Then I did another one and a third one. Now I'm going to a fourth one because of the quality of the submissions in the third book. We have four of the short stories/novelettes get considered for the Nebula and one of the stories (congratulations, Jonathan Brazee!) actually made the Nebula's final ballot. How about that for exposure for all the authors within?

Usually exposure leads to frostbite and dying of hunger, but as authors, we need to get our names out there and keep them out there. That's why politicians will put their name everywhere before an election. They want you to look at the ballot and remember that you've seen that name somewhere.

That is what makes ads important, which goes to backlist. I run AMS ads on all of my books. At least one ad, usually three or four because I want readers to constantly see my name and my books. Someone with that kind of backlist must be doing something right. Let me pick up one of his books.

So keep writing. Build your backlist. There are top authors with only six or seven novels published—A.G. Riddle comes to mind. First, write an incredible book, and second, the longer it's out there before the next one comes out, the more you're going to have to spend on ads to keep the sales up. And then spend more and more until you hit an equilibrium. Eventually, you are going to have to publish a new book to remain viable or you'll run out of ad cash, whichever comes first.

Here is a two-week pie chart of my backlist earnings as shown by the BookReport dashboard. Each one of the slices is revenue.

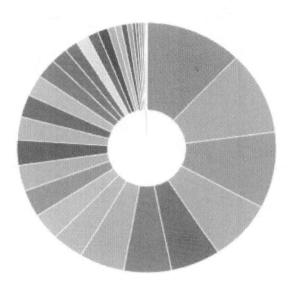

That pie chart does not include sixteen collaborations because it only shows books that I personally published through my KDP dashboard. It also doesn't include other revenue streams such as audiobooks (I have seventeen different books as audiobooks as of this writing) or paperbacks (I have all my books made into paperbacks because I love being able to hold my own stories).

Let's talk about paperbacks. I spent a career in Marine Corps Intelligence. Everything I did was a secret. Every report I wrote, every briefing I gave. I retired with a chest full of medals and not a single thing that I had written. Working as a business consultant, I liked being able to see a final product, like the aircraft carrier USS Gerald R. Ford. I got to work with the people building that ship and it was great. When I started writing, I knew that I would make paperbacks because I finally got to hold something in my hand that I made.

And there we are. My paperbacks pay for themselves because I have enough fans who only buy books in print, but it's not a windfall. As an indie, I can make a decision that I'll continue making paperbacks as long as I keep writing because I can do that. I am responsible only to my myself and that is a great feeling.

Keep writing. Keep filling that shelf. A thousand words a day every day for a year means you've written four nice length books. Keep doing that and pretty soon, you'll have a pie chart that looks like mine—every book contributing to your bottom line.

Improving your word count

I was a tried and true pantser, flying by the seat of my pants, telling the story as my fingers hit the keys. For more than two years I did it that way, but then I got busy. Running author conferences and managing a publishing empire (with enough titles, just changing the back matter takes a full day), I needed to increase my word count while my available time to write decreased.

First, write every day. There's nothing like practice to get better at something.

Second, outline! I know, this is me, and I'm suggesting you write an outline. It makes the story easier to write. Easier means quicker. When I have a moment of exceptional clarity, I will put everything else aside and write the story. It will be a series of events, snippets of conversation, bullet points of things, with lots of "and then." It will by heavily infested with typos and whatever. The only thing that matters is that I now have a complete story, anywhere from 2k to 10k words. When I sit down to write the book, I can jam it out and the first draft is pretty good. I managed to write the last book in two weeks because I had an outline. I think this will be my new norm. The important point is when a story comes to you and you see it all in your mind, get it down right then. As a full-time author, it's so much easier for me to put everything else aside and work on the outline.

If you have a day job? That's more problematic, but if you have a recorder on your phone, tell the story there. Skip lunch if you have to. You'll figure out what you meant to say between bites of your peanut butter sandwich. The sacrifices we make for our art, which then becomes a business. You'll be amazed at the leaps and bounds you can make when you have the story and just need to chip away at it. I can type 1500 to 2000 words an hour with a good outline. Sure, I flesh out the scenes, go back and forth to add three dimensions—the senses, the colors, those things that bring a scene to life—but the main story rips through.

It doesn't take too many of those hours before you have a full manuscript in your hand. Maximize your productivity while minimizing your time investment. Sounds like a business premise.

What I found is that a story written like that flows better and reads better from the outset. My editor makes fewer corrections, and my beta readers complained that I was trying to put them out of business because there were so few typos remaining. I like improving the quality of my words, but that didn't happen overnight or easily.

It took writing. A lot of writing. After two and a half million words, my first draft is pretty good and with that high-speed outline (not a real outline, just a story stripped to the barest of bones), then I can get those out quickly and with high quality.

You know who the best judge of quality is? Your readers. Not other authors. I figured out why the quality over quantity debate continues to rage between some authors. They are trying to denigrate others because of their own inability to deliver a quality manuscript quickly, which isn't a condemnation of anyone. I have practiced long and hard to get to this point. Did you ever believe that someone could run a mile in four minutes? Maybe you grew up knowing nothing but the four-minute mile.

I didn't. It took that first man to break the mark and then others followed quickly. You have to believe. And you have to train to meet a higher standard.

And the only thing that matters to you as an indie is what you yourself do. You can only control what you do, not what anyone else does. You shouldn't see what they do as a denigration of anything you do. If you think they do something better than you that you'd like to accomplish, work toward it. You can get there. You can write better.

You can write faster. You can do whatever you believe you can do by working hard at the right things. It may not come next week or next month—hell, maybe not even next year—but the only one who can hold an indie back is the indie.

Remember that part where you are in charge of everything you do? There you go. Break's over. Time to get back to work.

Social Proof

How do you know if your book is any good? Can strangers tell you? Will family tell you their truth, or will they say they love it because you wrote it?

It starts with a cover that aligns into the genre of the readers you're targeting. If you write westerns and science fiction readers are picking up and panning your book, that has nothing to do with your writing. That has everything to do with your marketing.

When your sales are low, like most authors have as they first start out, your friends and family will drive your Amazon "also boughts," the books that people buy who also bought your book. This happened with one of my books.

The number four book was *How to Knit Clothes Using Your Cat's Own Hair*. That wasn't very helpful for readers who picked up that book and saw my science fiction book as one of their recommendations.

For social proof to matter, it has to come from your book's genre. Maybe you cross multiple genres and you believe your book should appeal to a broader audience. I like to think my Free Trader series applies to cat lovers as well as science fiction fans. This has proved right over time, but not something I thought of when I first published the book. Same thing with Young Adult. The Free Trader has little sex and not graphic in any way, and no swearing. I tagged it for thirteen and up. Reviews told me it was YA. So I rebranded it, targeted new ad campaigns, and my sales increased dramatically.

Reviews can tell you a lot about your book. Someone might write a better blurb than you as part of their review. I have no shame. I'll use their words if theirs are a better hook than what I have.

Even if you get five stars, read what they say and what they don't say. Many authors don't read their reviews at all. I suggest you can learn a lot, like why I needed to rebrand the Free Trader as YA.

You need ten reviews if you want to run promotions on some of the sites like Robin Reads or ENT. Outside of that, reviews don't give you anything tangible. You don't get an improved book ranking. Amazon doesn't promote your book more just because you have fifty or one hundred reviews. What reviews show is that people liked your book and went out of their way to drop a few stars your way. I see one hundred as a magic number, then one thousand. A book with a thousand reviews is a big deal. In my experience, I get about one review for every fifty to one hundred books sold.

Social proof. When the right readers read your book, they'll tell you what they liked. Do more of that. If people are hesitant to give you feedback, then they probably didn't like the book. Find out, fix it, and move on.

In other words, write the next book. The things I love to see most in reviews are "well written" and "can't wait for the next one." I've done my job and with each new book, sales increase. That is a great feeling.

Staying Motivated (without alienating your family)

Writer's fatigue happens, whether you've had poor sales, bad reviews, or even something as simple as you're tired of typing (or dictating). Maybe you think you don't have any new stories to tell.

I can tell you what works for me. A new story, a short story with a fun plot or an odd twist. Those seem to flow for me. I can write one in one to two days, 5k to 8k words.

How about outlining a story? How about brainstorming? I'll step back and write dialogue, something that I always find fascinating. I might design a cover, which just needs the perfect story behind it.

If your main work is giving you fits, step back. Jim Butcher said, "I don't have writer's block. I have a mortgage." The work you don't do today is the money you don't get two or three months from now.

But fear isn't a proper motivator. You become less creative when you work from fear. The words are hard to come by and are painful to get onto the page.

Step back. Close your eyes, and think about why you started writing. The imaginary world. The story. The colors and the emotions. The turn of phrase to paint a word picture. Whatever it is, disappear into that moment. Write down that outline, that scene, that story. When your mind is clear and in a different place, go back to your main work and look at it from a third-party neutral perspective. Why was it causing you grief? Was it this work? Discover the reasons you are having trouble.

If the story isn't working, then figure out why. That nagging feeling you have is your conscience telling you something. You only have to listen closely to hear what it is.

If it's a new book and you don't know how it's supposed to go, I can't help you. Writers tell stories. If you don't have a story, then what will you tell? The beginning, the middle, and the end.

I write the first chapter and then I write the last chapter. I go back to write everything in between. Knowing how it ends helps me to frame the steps to get there. I have a rough outline in mind with three subplots. I've written from one point of view to nine. The more there are, the more sticky notes I need on my white board.

Don't despair, because there is always something to write next. I heard that James Patterson has thousands of rough plots in a closet full of notebooks. That is what you do when you're not writing. All the stories haven't been told yet.

I talked about goals. If you have a goal that your first book is a bestseller and allows you to retire on a beach somewhere, reality suggests that your first book won't even break even until after your third book comes out as long as all three are in the same genre.

I broke even on my first science fiction book exactly six months after I published it, after the sixth book in the series was published. So don't let the lack of instant success hold you back. Do you know who Hugh Howey is? *Wool* was his tenth book. It was a runaway blockbuster.

Finally, he realized success.

A couple other things you can try. Why sit and stare at the computer screen for hours on end? Give yourself a shorter overall writing period, sprinkled with sprints. Then get caught up on your recreational reading. See how other authors craft their words. Once you've written a book, you'll notice that you read differently, you look at things with a more critical or more accepting eye.

As a creative person, losing motivation is a real issue. You simply cannot let it go on for too long. Remember what this whole book is about. Control what you are in control of. Writing isn't just something to do, it's something you love to do. You can never let it become work, even though it's your job, but it's the fun part of your job.

Treat it that way and use writing as your escape from everything else.

Hitting the Wall

What do you do when you lose your motivation? Sales are lacking. No one likes your books. You're not getting reviews. You're writing and writing and no one appreciates any of it. And it's not bringing in any revenue.

I suck!

The demon of crippling self-doubt affects nearly all of us at some point. It is real. As an author, you are a creative. It is a challenge to turn your imagination on and off, and then take those scenes and turn them into words. It is the storyteller's challenge. As the production side of your business, you need to get the words down, otherwise there is no story to sell.

Do you have to sell the next story and you don't have it written? It's not flowing and you are going to miss your deadline?

Take a break and do something else. Explore marketing. There are hundreds of YouTube videos to help you. Buy a KU membership. For $10, you can reference a hundred books on marketing and the indie business.

One thing you can't do is nothing. If depression is gripping you and holding you down, then only you know what can bring you out of that, whether it's professional help, a distraction, or something else that has worked in the past.

To get the creative juices flowing, Thoreau had Walden's Pond. Sheldon Cooper (*Big Bang Theory*) did the mindless task of a busboy at Penny's restaurant until the idea hit him. There's a lot to be said for physical fitness, too. Being healthy is the best way to stay healthy. You need to feel right to write.

The Value of Time

Two years ago as a lawyer/business consultant, I billed at $250/hour and was gone from home half of my life. Fifteen months ago, I was making 12-14 cents/hour, but I was home. Now, an hour of my author time is worth well over $500.

But I'm inefficient with my time because I can be. Those who work full-time jobs and have young families at home don't have the luxury of wasting one minute. You have to do everything for your small business as an indie, which means you need to be efficient if you want to maximize your earnings potential.

What are your priorities to maximize your time?

#1 Writing. You are the talent, and you should always treat the talent right.

#2 Presentation. Preparing your book for market—cover, blurb, keywords, categories, reader engagement.

#3 Marketing. Books generally don't sell themselves. This includes your newsletter.

#4 Other Stuff. This is the admin, taxes, running your knuckles over a cheese grater, you know, the usual author stuff.

I'm not telling you anything you haven't heard before. You have to write the book and make sure that the cover and blurb help to sell it. If you don't do those first two things, you'll waste a great deal of time and money on marketing.

When you have the writing and presentation squared away to the best of your ability, then marketing becomes number one. I say that nothing sells the last book like the next book, but without some marketing, people won't know that last book exists, let alone the next one.

If you only have five hours a week in which to do it all and you're able to get a book a year published, I salute you! Making the most of your time is important. What brought this to the fore for me was having to edit a 60k word book (not mine) on a new story line that was my responsibility. I thought it would take three days and throw me way behind. It took thirteen hours, a little more than one work day, because I gave it my 100% focus. No Facebook, no writing, no marketing, no ka-ching from BookReport. (That's nice, but it's a distraction that you don't need unless you are doing hour-to-hour marketing, same thing with checking your author rank—if it doesn't change what you're doing at the moment, then you don't need to check it.)

Learn what you need to know at that particular time in your journey. If you haven't written your first book yet, there's no need to get overwhelmed by the marketing. Work on your craft until you need to know how to do a blurb. Research covers in your genre to make sure your cover attracts the right readers. When your book is done and getting ready to publish, study up on marketing. There's enough information available in various Facebook author groups (I would always recommend 20Booksto50k first) that you'll get a healthy start and be able to ask smarter questions, dial in the knowledge that will help you best at this particular time.

If you focus and prioritize, going after your number one with fanatical devotion, you'll find that you're able to get more from your time.

There are a couple rules of consulting. You can never have more than one priority one and when your number one issue is resolved, number two becomes number one—as in, you will always have something at the top of your list.

Give your top priority the attention it deserves, and you'll be amazed at what you can accomplish.

SEVEN

MARKETING

- Return on Investment
- Margin
- Amazon Ads
- Facebook Ads
- BookBub Ads

Overview

Very few people can be successful in this business without advertising. Most of those have built their followers over time and get a set number of sales with each new release. Some can make $100k/month based on the quality of their newsletter subscribers alone. I know one author who spends a relative pittance (a couple hundreds of dollars a month) in advertising and makes six figures month in, month out. She sells her readers two high-quality books a month and they buy the books when they are released. This is the epitome of the game.

I saw an ad on Amazon for *Harry Potter and the Sorcerer's Stone*. JK Rowling thinks she needs to advertise (at least her marketing team believes that there are more buyers out there), so why wouldn't the average Joe?

That's me. The blue collar author. I am your average Joe driven to succeed, a workaholic who believes that if I just work a little harder... It's better to work smarter, and it's far more lucrative.

I need to write the books because my readership is waiting impatiently, but these are good books with appeal to a far broader audience. Can I keep my readership happy while increasing my sales? How can I get my books into new hands? Marketing.

It is easier to sell ten books to one person than one book to ten, but I'm trying to do both because that is a whole new plateau up the mountain of success.

You're making the same face that I'm making. Advertising and marketing isn't hard, it only takes a little effort and thanks to the work of a few of my friends, it isn't even that much effort.

They have written entire books on some very specific details as well as provided most of the information at no cost on their Facebook pages or their blogs.

I'm not going to try to shortcut their work, because I'd end up quoting huge sections. I can't do that to them. I will tell you to buy their books as the current seminal works on the subject. Their books are what I use, and for this section, I'll go into how I use the advertising on those platforms.

Let's get some basic terms down first.

Money – at the end of the day, this is what we're talking about. We want more money at the end of every day than when we started.

Revenue – this is your gross earnings, how much money your book brings in. A $2.99 book in KDP Select will earn you roughly $2 in revenue.

Expense – a valid cost, even if it isn't tax-deductible, although we want all expenses to be tax-deductible.

Profit – what's left after you subtract the expenses from revenue. This is your "you" money.

Cash Flow – the money flowing in each month balanced

against the outflow. The money you make today on Amazon will be paid in two to three months. The money you spent on ads is paid at the end of the month, or in $500 chunk increments during the month. Pay me now, but you get paid later.

Overhead – these are your base costs that you have regardless of whether you publish a book or not.

Margin – this is how much you get between your cost and price.

There are people who borrow money to run ads. Until you are sure what kind of return on investment you'll get, I would be wary of spending more than I make, unless you know you can afford to take the loss. I wouldn't recommend spending much money at all on advertising until you have three books out. That's simply my opinion.

As I said before, it's so much easier to sell ten books to one person. Hold that mantra and start making money at this thing we call self-publishing. Once you figure out how to sell your books to one person, take what you learned and sell to two, then five, then ten, and keep building that foundation from which you can keep climbing.

Return on Investment (ROI)

This is one of the single most important calculations you can make. How much did you spend and how much did you make? If you can correlate these two efforts, then you can take steps to put your ad money into efforts that see you get two to three times your money back or more.

Primary ROI is when you put your book up for sale, see how much you spent on ads, and how much you made above your baseline. Did you make more than you spent?

An example. Your $2.99 book goes to 99 cents as part of a Kindle Countdown Deal. (One shortcoming is that this is US and UK only if you've set it up in both stores, but that's it.) Your royalty from each sale is 70 cents. If you bought a BargainBooksy ad, an Ereader News Today ad, a Robin Reads ad, and then boosted a few FB posts, you might be out $250.

$250 divided by $0.70 is 357.14. You need to sell 358 copies of your book before you are in the black and have a positive ROI. If you only have one book out, your entire profitability is based on how many copies you can sell of that one book above your costs.

But if you have more books in the series, then you will get your secondary ROI, which requires a series of calculations. In Michael Cooper's book, he has a spreadsheet and everything you need to make the calculations, but they go something like this.

If you have a 90% read-through (also called buy-through or pass-through rate) to book two, and 90% to book three, and so on to book ten, you can calculate how much money you will make from putting book one into someone's hands. If you make one dollar on each of your books from two through nine, then your revenue guesstimate will look something like this based on your 99 cent book one. All values are profits.

Ten copies of book one - $7.00

Nine copies of book two - $9.00 (because we have a 90% read-through, which means for every ten sales of book one, we'll have nine of book two)

Ninety percent to book three - $8.10

Ninety percent to book four - $7.29

Ninety percent to book five - $6.56

Ninety percent to book six - $5.90

Ninety percent to book seven - $5.31

Ninety percent to book eight - $4.78

Ninety percent to book nine - $4.30

Ninety percent to book ten - $3.87

Even with 90% read-through, you lose readers with each new book for whatever reason. Once you get up toward 100%, then you have the readership hooked solid.

If we have 90% read-through from book one and for the rest of the series, for every copy of book one that we sell, we don't make 70 cents, we make $6.21. Keep in mind the above calculations are for ten book one copies sold. It made the math look cleaner.

How much can you spend on book one and still make a profit? That's right—about six dollars. What if you break even on that first book in a series with your promotion? Then it's all gravy after that. That is the power of a backlist and a long series. If you don't write in a series, but you have a distinctive style within the same genre, then you can still get those readers to buy your other books. Use your back matter to highlight enough of a similarity—readers of my Free Trader will love Hades 7 or The Outcast!

Put on your production foreman, IT specialist, legal officer, and marketing guru hats for all the stuff in your book that isn't the actual story. Give people the opportunity to sign up for your newsletter or buy your next book. The power of eBooks is that once you have your next book, you can update the last book with link. Nothing like selling the next book as soon as the reader finishes the current one.

One word of caution for people who are wide. None of the booksellers like seeing links within your book to other booksellers' websites. Apple will reject a book with an Amazon link and Amazon will turn a book away with a Nook link and so on. You can use a universal link that is user-directed, where a Barnes & Noble fan will always get the link to B&N.

Sometimes booksellers don't like the random link. They can't tell if it's malware or not. Just be advised that you may not be able to have active links in your book, so having something that's easy to remember and easy to type for a reader is important. My landing page is craigmartelle.com. That's as easy as I could make it and maintain my brand.

Back to selling your books. Calculate your ROI correctly. With my backlist, if I can bring a single person on board who loves all my books, that is worth a minimum of $50 in profit. Money in the bank.

Sometimes things get tricky when you drill deeper into the numbers.

Many times, you will stack your ads along with newsletter swaps. You'll get a great payback but won't be able to put your finger on the payback for each individual promotion. That is known as throwing mud at the wall and seeing what sticks. It's okay. It's how most people do it, including me. I stack all my promotions, but I have an idea of what works better than others because I usually spread promotions across five days. Why five? Because Amazon lets me make a book free for five days each quarter.

I do that and will start promotions on the second day. Just in case there's a glitch on the first day, I can get the book to free before it starts. I'll send my NL on the first day once free is confirmed. I'll know what kind of response I get out of the gate because that will be the only promotion I run on the first day. Some of my Kindle Unlimited readers will pick up a book for free just to have it. They've already read it in KU, so in essence, I've already been paid for it by those good people. If not, then I hope they'll dive into the rest of the series after reading number one.

And that's where your secondary ROI comes from. It is all simply ROI, but I thought it would be easiest to explain by primary and secondary.

Margin

From a business perspective, margin is what you make on each book. A 99 cent book is worth about 35 cents. What if you could sell that same book for $4.99? It would be around $3.49 (assuming no delivery costs, but Amazon charges you for that if you use the 70% royalty option—the more megabytes your book is, the bigger slice Amazon takes). Can you move the same number of copies at $4.99? Isn't that the million-dollar question.

There's the Walmart model where you sell a bazillion of something at a low margin or the Lamborghini model where you sell very few of something but at a high margin.

We are going to be far closer to the Walmart model, but as you are able to command higher prices, then you'll strike a balance with a better margin and high sales. That's where you'll find the seven-figure authors.

They didn't get there overnight or through any shortcuts.

Amazon Marketing Services (AMS) Ads

I use AMS ads and I can't get them to spend all of the money I put out there, but don't be dissuaded! There are plenty of horror stories where AMS, out of the blue, spent everything that a person had put in regards to a maximum. I keep my daily total bids fairly low across a vast number of ads. They won't max out all of them at one time. In a couple years of advertising using AMS, they have not even come close. I'm currently spending only $15/day, but am willing to spend $100 as long as the commensurate sales happen.

I have between one and two hundred AMS ads running at any point in time. I use a combination of automatic targeting and manual targeting. For quick and easy exposure and low-cost engagement, I run automatic ads on all my books. I set the CPC at $0.25 and the daily at $3 unless it starts getting impressions and then I might crank it up to $10 or $20. AMS has never spent all my money, but they could. Be aware.

Mastering Amazon Ads by Brian Meeks:

- My Book for the eBook
- My Book for the paperback.

Facebook (FB) Ads

Facebook will happily take your poorly allocated money. All of it. You need to do better than that. Good news! My friend Michael Cooper lives by the power of FB ads. Buy his book to learn the best way to do the foundational things. Then when you are making good money, you can test other ways.

Help! My Facebook Ads Suck by Michael Cooper:

- My Book for the eBook
- My Book for the paperback

Despite what Michael says, I do boost posts, but I have a number of target groups established. As FB restricted who they show posts to, I boost my author posts showing new releases so that the thousand people who follow me on that page will get to see my stuff! I usually boost for a week, most times for $20, but sometimes for $50. I haven't seen the difference by spending the extra $30. I think FB is smart enough that the ones I can get for $20 are the ones who click and buy. I also make it easy for them—I use the amazon link. One click and they are on Amazon's page, a mere hover away from a one-click buy.

BookBub Ads

David Gaughran's work on the subject: https://us2.campaign-archive.com/?u=7fa8f00bfd097735355723f4f&id=a2b1384ad3

What David tells you is that you start off targeting authors like you and then BB will run your ad based on the readers who follow those authors. Anyone with less than a thousand followers may not be a good target.

So I went to BookBub and looked at the top twenty military science fiction authors for a new campaign I was starting. What did I find? The Mil SciFi author with the greatest following had 786. Next had less than 500. Those guys! I only have 50. I hadn't been pushing that and was missing out, big time. I'm going to do two things. First, I'm going to keep promoting readers to follow me on BookBub so when I have a new release, BB will send it to those who follow me and it looks just like a Featured Deal! How can you beat that? Sounds like free money to me. I suck because I didn't take it seriously. But I am now. And second, I'm going to target a few of the Mil SciFi authors through a few test ads with fairly low spend to see who resonates and then I'm going to scale up my spend in hopes of scaling up the sales.

BookBub is another service that will happily spend all your money. Take great care with your advertising budget until you have things dialed in.

BB also has a great tutorial and blog that you can find what you need. It starts with a good graphic, an image that is 300 x 250 pixels—this is how you get people to give your book a shot. Having a number of them for testing will be helpful. Facebook ads reward pictures that don't look like ads (i.e. images without text on them). BB, not so much. You need to put a very short pitch. BB's blog is where you'll find good information.

https://insights.bookbub.com/

EIGHT

RANDOM STUFF, OTHER WORDS AND DEFINITIONS

- Author Rank
- Collaborating
- Bestseller Lists
- Conventions & Professional Organizations
- Random Rants

Author Rank

I used to watch my author rank like a hawk. It was great to see it climb, and a bummer to see it drop. It's a general barometer of author health. 10,000 overall is better than 100,000. To me, that means you have much greater exposure, more readers who can spread the word about your work. The difference between an author rank of 10,000 and 50,000 could be two book sales and five KU borrows. If the borrowers never read it, you made money on two sales. That's it.

The real exposure comes when you get into the top 100 of your genre. Readers can then see you as Amazon shows your author rank as well as the ranks of those around you. If you aren't in the top 100 of any genre, no reader will ever know what your author rank is.

How do you get there?

Publish books that people are willing to pay for.

People can see authors in the top 100 free as well as the top 100 paid. That is a marketing methodology because free books don't pay the bills, but free books could find you readers that can't put your books down. Are you writing those kinds of books? Do you hook them with that first sentence, that first page? The intro to your book is key and then you have to keep that momentum. World builders! Shine the flashlight on just what the readers need to know at that moment, draw them into the story, and then paint the world before their eyes.

And they'll end up paying for your other books. That's how your author rank climbs. Because your marketing campaigns expose readers to books that they can't put down.

Keep writing, keep improving, and keep doing what you have to in order to draw the readers in. If they aren't picking up book 2, then get your book to a developmental editor to see why. The feedback and what you do with it could help you become a household name.

If you give your book away for free, a 10% read-through to book 2 is reasonable. For a paid book 1, 50% is reasonable. If you are below those numbers, then get a critical look at your writing. You may find that you are not aligned with the genre you are targeting. Or there may be something more significant impacting your book. Fix it and move on.

Write that next book, because **nothing sells the last book like the next one.**

On a technical note, for Amazon, if you are in Kindle Select—meaning your book is in the Kindle Unlimited program and exclusive to Amazon—then you will get credit for a sale and a borrow in the same way. The bad news is if someone borrows your book but doesn't read it, you make no money. They need to borrow it, read it, and return it to get another one of your books.

A rule of thumb is that the closer your book gets to the top of the charts, the steeper the climb. To get to a ranking of 10,000 to 20,000, you only need to sell about ten to fifteen books a day. To get from 10k to 1000, you need to sell about a hundred, maybe more. That's your book rank. The highest that any of my books have gone is 105 and that was The Bad Company, a new military science fiction novel, first in a series, that sold nearly 1000 copies that first day. My author rank climbed to number 9 in science fiction and 280 overall.

In order to stay consistently in the top 1000, I have one or two books in the top 1000 rank, maybe ten to fifteen ranked less than 10k, and then another twenty or thirty that are in the top 50k rank. Those aren't eye-popping numbers, but they are the way the blue collar author approaches this business. Each new release generally jumps up to the 200 to 1000 rank and that keeps my author rank healthy.

And that's how you build your author rank.

The bottom line with author rank is that it is a general barometer of health. If you have a rank of less than one thousand and all your books are at full price, you are doing well. If your rank is based off a huge 99 cent promo, then maybe not so much. And rank doesn't matter for visibility until you get into the top 100 overall.

Although it's nice to be in the top 20 of my category, it has been well over a year since I was out of the top 100 in science fiction authors. I like that. I'm always on the list and in good company. I know most of the authors around me on that list, whether at number fifty, or number five. And even better, they know me. I like the hell out of that and that keeps me hungry to stay at the top of my game. I can't be putting out a book in the company of giants, can I? The readers think I am and they are buying my books and keeping me in the company of those science fiction authors whom I respect the most.

Collaborating

It's been about eighteen months and nearly $300k in royalties since Michael Anderle and I published the first book in our co-written series, the Terry Henry Walton Chronicles.

Michael built a readership that had a voracious appetite. He couldn't keep up with them, so looked to do a spin-off series. He picked Terry Henry Walton (THW) as a popular character with prime air-time in two of his books. And the stories had to fill a 150-year gap in time. He needed an author with a track record of writing post-apocalyptic novels, experience in the Marine Corps, and freakishly driven.

The collaboration was born. I put my ego aside and learned a great deal from Michael about character development and telling a compelling story. His readers were both gracious and demanding. I learned much from them too.

In the first six months, we published eight books with a total word count of 520,000 words, and five short stories totaling 10k words. I've paid my editor almost $3500 during that time. I do write full-time, so word count is one measure of that time. I also wrote a 90k book for one of my own series. In the year since, we've added almost another million words.

Collaborating is a testament to delivering a product in a way that any small business would. We meshed and were able to deliver with a velocity that worked for our readership. I say ours, because the readers know that I'm the primary author of this series, and they are okay with that. They've grown accustomed to my style, which was a little different from Michael's.

I'd like to think that I'm a better version of me today because of this collaboration. The series would have died with number two had we not hooked the readers. That is what the minimally viable product is all about. We took the reader feedback and went on a journey with them. Our read-through is about 90% once we get them through Book 2. We study the numbers and do what's best to keep the series foremost for existing readers while running ads to get it in front of new readers.

Success takes a great deal of work. Collaborating is one way to share the burden, but it still comes down to writing, learning, writing better, and then managing the business side. In the end, it's all worth it.

What other ways can you collaborate? How many varieties of

friendships are there? You can both write together, all the words, using an online environment like Google Docs. You could write one chapter back and forth. You write one, a partner writes one, then you dive back in and write one, and so on until the book is done. One person writes and the other punches it up, adding flavor and more.

You can build a world and others can write within that world.

You can create a world together. I know of one group that publishes under one pen name, but there are a bunch of them and they each write a book within their created universe. They release rapidly without any one person carrying an unequal burden.

And always use a contract in all collaborative efforts. Look at including the following things:

- Names of collaborators
- Time frame of inclusion, including publishing dates, where, and for how long
- Derivative rights (what if someone wants to make a movie or line of toys?)
- What happens if one of the collaborators passes away?
- Royalties and payments
- Who owns the IP, such as the work in progress?
- What about cutting ties? How can you walk away from the contract?
- Remedies – what happens if one party defaults on the contract (and go to court is not a valid statement, because you don't need a clause to challenge a contract in court. I'm talking automatic conversion of collaborative IP if payment isn't made or something like that)
- Editorial revisions and moral rights (can the publisher edit your work to such an extent that it is no longer your work?)

I'm not going to show a sample of one because once again, liability. Get a lawyer to review any contract to make sure you aren't signing your life away. You need to account for a number of things in the contract. Make sure you know what you're getting into.

Bestseller Lists

If you hit number one overall on Amazon's free list or number one in any category during a free promotion, it doesn't rate any banners. The key word in bestseller is "sell." If you hit number one in a category (one of over a thousand on Amazon), they may give you an orange tag that says "Bestseller." Take a screen shot of that, because you are now an Amazon Bestseller. I put those in my folder with that book and move on. I have folders for each separate book as a sub-folder of each series.

USA Today and Wall Street Journal use gross sales as their gauge of bestsellers and they list a bunch of books each week. They count the numbers from Monday through Sunday, retailers report on Monday or Tuesday, and the list posts Tuesday or Wednesday. If you hit one of those, congratulations!

NY Times is an editorial effort. There was a lawsuit about that from a person who sold some 30,000 copies of his book in a single week. He didn't make the list and took it all the way to the Supreme Court. NY Times won under the argument that the list is considered to be editorial in nature. Actual sales was irrelevant to what they posted. If you want to hit the NY Times list, you have that hurdle to cross in addition to a mass quantity of sales.

Conventions & Professional Organizations

There are a bunch out there and most have an annual fee attached, but it goes to a good cause.

I was surprised to find that there was no single resource for conventions online. The best thing to do is search for those who hold some sort of annual or regional event. Try these groups.

- Professional Organizations / Groups
- NINC (Novelists Inc)
- RWA (Romance Writers' Association)
- SFWA Nebula Conference (Science Fiction and Fantasy Writers of America)
- MWA (Mystery Writers of America)
- HWA (Horror Writers of America)
- SoA (Society of Authors)
- NWU (National Writers Union)
- SCBWI (Society of Children's Bookwriters and Illustrators)
- ALLi (Alliance of Independent Authors)
- 20Books (Vegas, Bali, Edinburgh – not for profit self-published author shows)
- MileHiCon (Denver)
- Norwescon (Seattle)
- DragonCon (Atlanta)

Does this list seem anemic? It is, because it's only a sample. Comic book conventions are huge, but how good do indies do at those shows? Not so well, I've heard, but your experience may be different. Make sure you are aligned with your readership and then find the conferences, conventions, and shows that fit.

Craft shows where you practice writing or work on the craft specific to your genre are also completely different. Most of these are paid services and I don't have firsthand knowledge from any of them, so I'm not going to post them here as I don't want it perceived that I support one over another, because I simply don't know. If you are looking at a paid service, do your due diligence. Research with past students and find out who has taken what they've learned and become successful. What are they teaching and to what extent?

Yes, here I am charging you for this eBook and talking about what others are doing by charging you. I only put this book together because a number of new authors wanted a reference of my general conversations. They said they would pick out what would help them the best. That fits with my mantra that no one can tell you how to take your journey. It is yours alone to power through the climb, but you can find things to help you and pitfalls to avoid. The challenge is to keep climbing until you reach your personal goal, then define a new one and head for that.

That's what this book is all about. It's not a step-by-step guide, even though I put "A Guide" on the cover. No one but you can determine which signposts will lead you to your destination.

Random Rants from the 20Booksto50k Facebook Group

When you have a gazillion authors in one place, sometimes they get a little rambunctious. As General George S. Patton, Jr. said, if you want them to remember it, give it to them dirty.

LANGUAGE WARNING! The last bit of this chapter is salted with a few F-bombs and other things that you may not want to read. Skip past if you need to. The bibliography is a nice piece of gear for research and further professional development.

I try not to go overboard and try not to swear too much in my daily life, but there are times when it gushes forth like water over the dam. Damn! Get that shit under control! Go outside, unfuck yourself, and then get back in here! What the hell?

In any case, because people asked for these, here they are. Random rants...

How do you maintain high quality and still publish quickly?

Writing a book takes time. You have to get the words down, they need to be good words with pace and flow, good characters, a compelling plot. I can do roughly 1000 words an hour of that. A 60k word book takes 60 focused hours. I spend 70-80 hours a week in front of my computer, so getting 20 focused hours per week is eminently doable because I do this full-time.

I can get 1500 words per hour during certain scenes, but I am best budgeting for 1000. With my new high-speed, low-drag, long-range, high-intensity, low-profile outlining technique I show below, I can get up to 1500 words per hour for almost any scene. I see my production increasing to crazy numbers.

I write a lot and just like anything, I have gotten better with practice. Just like you can't run a marathon the first time you strap on the sneakers, you probably won't knock out a high-quality book a month when you first start out. My goal initially was 1000 WPD and I didn't always hit it. Now, it is a sorry day if I can't get 2500 words. And I write every single day. You can't edit a blank page and that big bucket of nothing gets deep quickly if you don't write.

I listen to my editors. (I have a few.) I send partially completed manuscripts to my insiders for a sanity check. None of that happened overnight. It took a good year and a half of constant production and listening to the people who were trying to help (and who understood me). I also read my reviews looking for trends to help me address plot issues, although thanks to early checking by my editors, the general stories were sound and the characters were three-dimensional.

I have an editor on salary, another two on standby, developmental editors ready to help, and a small team of insider beta readers. I thank them all profusely every chance I get, even if I don't agree with their input. They took the time to give me their opinions and I listen. They have the perspective of readers, so my assumption is if they have to ask, then I wrote it wrong.

When I get edits back, I stop what I'm doing and address them—first editor, second editor, developmental editors, and finally, beta readers. Usually, that intervention takes from 15 minutes to an hour. Deal with it and move on.

I do all this in a continuous cycle. After nearly 2.5 million words, I send my first draft to my editor as soon as I type the end. Then I start the next book. While writing one book, if I have a moment of exceptional clarity, I will put everything aside and outline the whole new story—this is my new thing—even if it is only a 1000 words of outline. A good story starts with a great hook and wraps up with an awesome (and happy, for my readers) ending. I make sure to capture those. I'll add some dialogue tidbits, some scenes, some interactions, a general flow, some people use the term beats, but those only happen in my head. And there you go. Imagine. Write. Repeat.

The Danger of Moral Relativism - A Rant

If you are trying to be someone other than yourself, I recommend you stop.

Seriously. Fucking stop. How many words I write in a day is immaterial to how many you write in a day, which has no relation to whether they are good words or not. Only you can put the right number of good words on the paper each day.

What other people do doesn't matter to what you can do.

I post numbers and such, but only to show what's possible. You don't want to be me. I can't freaking breathe. Last night, I slept a few hours, got up for a couple, then grabbed another hour and a half of sleep. No one wants to live like that. I surely don't. I make the most of my time with what I have.

Which is all anyone can do. How do you plan your work? How do you prepare your story? How do you grind out the words, even when it's only background stuff between the good scenes? When it's done, how do you find people who will pay for it, like it, and then buy more of your stuff?

That's what this group is about. It is a smorgasbord, not a horse race where you have to become a thoroughbred. None of us are thoroughbreds here. We're all mutts, scrappy and refusing to leave the track when someone else tells us that we're not good enough.

It is your business. That doesn't mean someone won't tell you that your baby's ugly. We've all heard those words. Are they right? Many times they are, sometimes they aren't. No matter what, listen, and then adjust as only you can. Don't try to be someone else. If someone tells you to write more like James Patterson, then you'll be set.

Bullshit. Write like you, taking good lessons in craft from those who are dominating your genre, but always write in your voice. It could change over time. That's okay. We evolve as writers. I thank the stars that after two million words published, I don't write like I used to. My average sentence length was eight words. Holy crap! I think I do much better now, but that was on me to change and determine if I wanted to change.

No one else. Whether you publish one book a year or thirty, there are tips, hints, hacks, and best practices that can help you. It's a smorgasbord. Choose what's best for you and understand that sometimes, there are business consequences. You may hit it big with one book of poetry published once a year, but the odds are against it. By publishing often in a big market, I hedge my bet. If I wrote only one book a year, I doubt that I would make even $5k a year. That's the reality of my publishing business. But that's my business and the pressure to get out the next story is on me and me alone, but not because someone else is doing it, but because the fans want it.

We all want fans and when you get them, you cradle them in a fleece-lined basket. I write for me and I write for my fans. My last book, published on Christmas Day, has been my best-received book, highest consistent ranking, and best-reviewed. I took six weeks to write it and get it out, because that worked for my situation. The fans waited for me, because I stayed in touch with them, shared that I had the flu.

None of that stuff happened by accident. I spent two years building my newsletter subscribers, gaining followers on Amazon, earning the trust of my readers. This business is hard and I always encourage people to work hard at the right things.

"I'm down and don't feel like writing today." We all feel like that, but in this case, I would always encourage you to get a few words down. Write something. An author's safe place is their stories. It's where you can be yourself, if only for a few moments. You can't edit a blank page and you may delete your words later, but get something down, not because of others but because that's what professional authors do. They write the words. How many? That's up to you. Compare yourself to no one else.

We can all be envious of someone else's success, but that is where moral relativism rears its ugly head. It's where those who believe that if you write a book a month, they must be low quality. BULLSHIT! Speed and quality are not mutually exclusive. Many authors can do it. Many others cannot. What matters is what you can do. No one runs a marathon the first day they strap on the sneakers.

- Write every day and you'll be amazed at what you can accomplish.
- Get feedback on your craft from those in your genre, readers, because they are your target audience for sales.
- Improve with every new word, but only you know where your goal is.
- Listen, study, and put into practice those elements that will help you improve your sales.
- Set your goals by what is in your control. 'Make a million dollars' is not in your control, but incrementally applying marketing lessons from the likes of Brian Meeks and Michael Cooper is in your control.
- Most importantly, be the best version of yourself that you can be. It is far too bothersome trying to be someone else.

Book Length

See what I did there? Book is an undefined term. I publish lots of books, some are novels, others novellas, even some novelettes and short stories.

SFWA (Science Fiction and Fantasy Writers of America, even though it's a worldwide organization) has defined the terms with set word counts.

Novel - 40k plus words

Novella - 17,500 to 40k

Novelette - 7,500 to 17,499

Short Story - up to 7,499 words

What does this mean to you and the word count of your stories? I suggest that these limits are meaningless. What is the right word count for you and your story? What is the right business model to sell your product? (Remember: when you publish your book, it becomes a product.)

Try to get the right word count to the best business model that you can handle. Some genres sell well at 50k words. If you write a 150k word tome and put it up, it may not sell well or you may have to work extra hard at marketing and you may not be able to charge three times what the 50k word books sell for. Does it take three times as long to write? Are the production costs three times as much? (There's only one cover, but editing costs are usually by the word.)

Sometimes, you have to step outside of yourself and have that business conversation. I can't write a book under 100,000 words! That's fine, but understand the business impact. Maybe you need to write a 200k word book to fit into the epic fantasy genre, but your book is only 70k words. That's okay, too. Put on your business hat and determine how you will market it and what the test readers think of it. It's a product and not all products sell well, no matter how much we love them.

The reason I'm posting this is because many people have been lamenting word counts and asking what people write. There is little value in that. What does your specific genre look like? (That goes to reader expectations, which is what writing to market means.) If you go outside normal boundaries (and we are all about hacking the process here), understand that you will face business challenges. If you don't have a firm grip on marketing and such, you may not want to tackle that obstacle out of the gate. Once established, you may be able to define your own market. JK Rowling did that and it was well worth it once the market responded, but she had a team of professionals on her side. We're indies and have to carry that load ourselves or share a great deal of our profits with someone else who may or may not come through for us.

I published a post-apoc book (general genre length is 50k words) that was 117k words long. It did really well. It only took me an extra week to write the additional words (that was a great writing week), and the payout in KU page reads was tremendous. No lamentations here and the readers were stoked to get two books for the price of one, which was how we marketed it.

You have to write the story first. It helps to have a target in mind that you can get close to through a good outline and an idea what the reader expectations are for your genre. You could be like me and simply call everything you publish a book.

No fucking shortcuts!

If you can't tell, this might be a rant.

Being an indie is hard work and you get to do it all. Don't compare yourself to me and don't tell me I can't write good books because I write them too quickly. Just because you can't do this (yet), it doesn't mean it can't be done. I don't give a flying goat fuck what Agatha Christie did in the 1930s. When it comes to writing, I care what Craig Martelle can do in 2018. Period.

I share what I learn because in my past, I've hurt people. I have a lot to make up for. Have you ever killed anyone? Try to be a little more understanding on why someone might be fanatically driven, whether to help other people or to race up a mountain of publishing success. Or do both. Still, your journey is yours alone.

Learn from me. That's what wisdom is all about. I guarantee that I learned all these lessons the hard way. You don't have to do it wrong it in the first place. If you know where the pitfalls are, they are easier to avoid.

If you want to go on an epic nut roll, have at it. That's your business. My tolerance for people trying to drag others down to their level is at an end. This one-finger salute is for you. Just because you can't motherfucking do it doesn't mean it can't be done. What separates the winners from everyone else? Digging in, doing the hard work after everyone else has gone home, learning. As you write and publish, you will find a thousand people willing to coach you, just like everyone in the stands at every sporting event. Just because they are yelling different stuff, it doesn't make any of it wrong. Listen and learn.

What did I do to get to this place? I worked a job for the first 21 years of my life so I could have health care for life and a retirement. Those gave me the foundation to do other things, like put myself through law school so I could make some real money in order to set myself up for enjoying life. Finally, at age 52, everything was in place for me to do what I wanted to do. I couldn't have done it at 22, or 32, or even 42 (age 42—that's when I started law school, graduating summa cum laude 2 ½ years later).

Everyone's path is different because everyone's motivation is different because everyone's goal is different. 20Booksto50k is about doing what needs to be done to make money. If you want to write the next literary masterpiece, I congratulate you for embracing that goal. It may take a number of tries, but if you want it badly enough, go after it. If you want to make money, it'll be hard if you don't enjoy writing the stories, like crawling through broken glass hard. People talk about writing to market. That is simply finding the balance between what you like to write and where people are buying the stories. You may be able to snag a bestseller in a small market, but will you be able to make a living? That's your business to determine which is most important.

I'm personally okay with a book ranked 200 overall on Amazon that isn't a bestseller as opposed to one ranked 2000 that is. That's my personal preference.

You can make a good living writing two or four books a year, but you better embrace marketing, good ads, and business management. If you only want to write, then accept that you may not make a living wage. The vast majority of authors don't. Once again, 20Booksto50k is about tips, hints, tricks, and lessons to help you sell more books, but you have to find what works best for you.

70-80 hours every fucking week. I have averaged 2664 words per day, every single day, for the past 876. Yes, I keep track to that level of fidelity because I embrace the business side as much as the storytelling side. I'm going to Iceland for a week in May and then Bali in January. Those are my vacations and if you're up on things, you'll know Bali is a conference, but it'll be a total bash, authors sitting around and talking, enjoying adult beverages, maybe getting some sun on the beach, but most of all, meeting, greeting, and celebrating. That is my idea of a vacation because when it comes to the author biz, I'm all in.

And that didn't happen overnight. There's no shortcut to stardom. There's no shortcut to Hollywood. There's no shortcut in writing a book. You and you alone have to do the work. Surrounding yourself with good people helps lighten the load, but you still have the heavy lifting.

The bottom line of this rambling diatribe is that you need to temper your goals with what you are willing and capable of doing. Not everyone is going to get to be a full-time author and very few of those will reach atmospheric levels of success. I work hard at the right things and I am rewarded in multiple ways—meeting great people, having people talk about their success based on lessons from this group, selling more books, and getting incredibly supportive reviews and comments. Sure, I work really hard, not all of it pans out, but this is the best job I've ever had and it wouldn't have been possible without all the other jobs that I've had.

Rational Discourse (a RANT)

I don't get angry on here often because I believe that most people are good people trying to do a little better for themselves and their families with each new day.

20Books is something I wholeheartedly believe in. So much so that I've committed hundreds of hours of my time and nearly $10,000 of my money to put on two conferences, with the potential for annual shows going forward.

That all depends on the base premise that people can share WHAT WORKS FOR THEM! Don't dictate to others what they should or shouldn't do. Everyone is at a different stage of their journey. Everyone needs a different tool to help them get over the next hump. That's what the 20Books conferences are trying to do—you sit back, take what you can from the presentations, network with people who you can relate to, and go back home to put those lessons into practice.

Insisting that someone use the Oxford comma is FUCKING MORONIC! If you use it, fine! That's your business. Telling someone else to use it isn't what this group is all about.

This group is about how to make money off what we love to do! If your books aren't selling, telling other people that their writing isn't good enough doesn't make readers buy your books. BUT THERE IS A SHITLOAD OF TIPS IN HERE THAT WILL HELP!

Craft is one part of what we do. If you don't take that seriously, then there may be some long-term viability issues with your product. Make no mistake, your stories are a product to be sold. If you don't think so, then you shouldn't be in this group. You're not selling your baby! It's a story and you can love it, but when you publish it, it's a product.

I am a huge fan of continuous improvement. Your first book can be total shit, but if people see the story within and want to read more, then you know you are onto something. Michael calls that the minimal viable product. Story trumps the Oxford fucking comma. Get better with each new book and the readers will take the journey with you.

With over 10,000 members in 20Booksto50k, it would be easy to destroy what this group is about through petty dictates. Don't fall into that trap. If you share, share what works for you. If you comment, comment what works for you—a little educated rhetoric goes a long way. Name-calling does not. Denigration does not. This group is about support in a shark-filled publishing world with indies out there on their own, fighting against the big money of trad pub.

A rising tide lifts all boats. Continue on your PERSONAL journey up the mountain to more and more profitability as an author. Fill your toolbox as you go with tips as you find them, and for FUCK'S SAKE PEOPLE, be decent human beings.

And this wasn't about the Oxford comma, for fuck's sake. The comments were out of control on this rant, which only solidified my point, but not to those who needed to hear it.

BIBLIOGRAPHY

As books from these good people change over time, I'm going to list just the main ones that I have. Check out their Amazon author page to see what else they have in their bag of supporting tricks.

Brian Meeks
  Mastering Amazon Ads, @2017.
  https://www.amazon.com/dp/B072SNXYMY
  Brian's Author Page on Amazon
  https://www.amazon.com/Brian-D.-Meeks/e/B0073XZH78

David Gaughran
  Let's Get Digital: How to Self-Publish and Why You Should, @2018
  https://www.amazon.com/dp/B078ZNWD61
  From Strangers to Superfans, @2018
  https://www.amazon.com/gp/product/B0798PH9QT/
  David's Author Page on Amazon
  https://www.amazon.com/David-Gaughran/e/B004YWUS6Q

BIBLIOGRAPHY

Honoree Corder with Ben Hale
    Write Like a Boss
    https://www.amazon.com/gp/product/B0765MGBHF/
    Publish Like a Boss
    https://www.amazon.com/gp/product/B0785L1X2R/
    Market Like a Boss
    https://www.amazon.com/gp/product/B079KX7S9K/
    Honoree's Author Page
    https://www.amazon.com/Honoree-Corder/e/B005DO6BPQ

Michael Cooper
    Help! My Facebook Ads Suck
    https://www.amazon.com/dp/B078NBW3M3/
    Michael Cooper's Author Page
    https://www.amazon.com/Michael-Cooper/e/B071FJHK9K

Chris Fox
    5000 Words Per Hour
    https://www.amazon.com/dp/B00XIQKBT8/
    Write to Market
    https://www.amazon.com/dp/B01AX23B4Q/
    Six Figure Author
    https://www.amazon.com/dp/B01LZEM7SB/
    Relaunch Your Novel
    https://www.amazon.com/gp/product/B071HVZD1G/
    Chris's Author Page
    https://www.amazon.com/Chris-Fox/e/B00OXCKD2G

Chris Syme
    Sell More Books with Less Marketing
    https://www.amazon.com/dp/B071P7VG7S/
    Chris Syme's Author Page
    https://www.amazon.com/Chris-Syme/e/B0084PYSYW

BIBLIOGRAPHY

Bryan Cohen
    How to Write a Sizzling Synopsis
    https://www.amazon.com/dp/B01HYBWOF6/
    Bryan's Author Page
    https://www.amazon.com/Bryan-Cohen/e/B004I9WJTY

Dave Chesson, Kindlepreneur
    Book Marketing 101 & KDP Rocket
    https://kindlepreneur.com/book-marketing-101/
    Amazon Book Description Generator Tool
    https://kindlepreneur.com/amazon-book-description-generator/

Mark Dawson
    Learn Amazon Ads
    https://www.amazon.com/dp/B06Y6BSRLR/
    Mark's Author Page
    https://www.amazon.com/Mark-Dawson/e/B0034Q9BO8
    Mark's outstanding Self-Publishing Formula course - https://selfpublishingformula.com/

Maxwell Alexander Drake
    Dynamic Story Creation in Plain English: Drake's Brutal Writing Advice
    https://www.amazon.com/dp/B01IGSWNIO/
    Point of View – Better Writing through Stronger Narrative
    https://www.amazon.com/dp/B073NRJKPT/
    Drake's Author Page
    https://www.amazon.com/Maxwell-Alexander-Drake/e/B006QP41O4

Shawn Coyne
    The Story Grid: What Good Editors Know @2015
    https://www.amazon.com/dp/B00WT7TP8A/

BIBLIOGRAPHY

Tim Grahl
    Your First 1000 Copies
    https://www.amazon.com/dp/B00DMIWAIC/
    Tim's Author Page
    https://www.amazon.com/Tim-Grahl/e/B00DN6ZH38

Rachel Aaron
    2k to 10k: Writing Faster, Writing Better, and Writing More of What You Love
    https://www.amazon.com/dp/B009NKXAWS/
    Rachel's Author Page
    https://www.amazon.com/Rachel-Aaron/e/B004FRLQXE

Joe Solari
    Business Owner's Compendium: A practical guide to the theory of starting, owning and operating a business
    https://www.amazon.com/dp/B0728G3T7N/
    Joe's Author Page
    https://www.amazon.com/Joe-Solari/e/B01MZ4KOPM

James Baldwin
    Fix Your Damn Book! A self-editing guide for authors – how to painlessly self-edit your novels and stories
    https://www.amazon.com/dp/B01FQOI1P0/
    James' Author Page
    https://www.amazon.com/James-Osiris-Baldwin/e/B00J4OHNGC

Scott King
    The Five Day Novel
    https://www.amazon.com/dp/B01MDN3015
    Outline Your Novel
    https://www.amazon.com/dp/B079QN8FGK
    Scott's Author Page

https://www.amazon.com/Scott-King/e/B002BMAE9C

Rhett C. Bruno & Steve Beaulieu
    Two Authors, One Book: Co-Writing
    https://www.amazon.com/dp/B07BMKLKC4

Tammi Labrecque
    Newsletter Ninja: How to Become an Author Mailing List Expert
    https://www.amazon.com/gp/product/B07C6J8HP9
    Tammi's Author Page
    https://www.amazon.com/Tammi-Labrecque/e/B00Q7RSPEI/

APPENDIX A

Acronyms used in Become a Successful Indie Author

ACX – Audiobooks on Amazon
AMS – Amazon Marketing Services (Amazon ads)
BB – BookBub (the gold standard paid newsletter promotion service)
ENT – eReader News Today (a paid newsletter promotion service)
KDP – Kindle Direct Publishing
KENP – Kindle Edition Normalized Page (count)
KU – Kindle Unlimited
ML – Mailing List
NL - Newsletter

APPENDIX B

SYNONYMS FOR SAID, YELL, & MOVE

Synonyms for said, yell, and move. Don't overuse anything and don't break the flow inserting a synonym. Many times, 'said' is the right word to use. I offer these simply as something to think about. Remember, there is no one right way and don't let anyone tell you something different.

APPENDIX B

Said

accounted
alleged
announced
answered
articulated
assumed
barked
blubbered
blurted
called
chided
claimed
commanded
communicated
compared
complained
conjectured
considered
countered
cried
croaked
declared
deemed
demanded
droned
estimated
exclaimed
expressed
gossiped
griped
growled
grumbled
grunted
held
hissed
instructed
intonated
intoned
joked
lectured
mentioned
moaned
mouthed
murmured
muttered
narrated
offered
ordered
phonated
pleaded
pronounced
put into words
quipped
reckoned
recounted
regarded
relayed
replied
reported
requested
responded
retorted
rumored
said
scoffed
seeming
shot back
snapped
snarled
sneered
sniveled
snorted
sobbed
sounded
squeaked
stated
sung
supposed
taunted
thought
told
uttered
verbalized
vocalized
voiced
wept
whimpered
whined
whispered
yelped

Asked

Requested
Queried
Questioned
Wondered

Yelled

Bellowed	Screeched
Hollered	Shouted
Howled	Shrieked
Roared	Wailed
Screamed	Yowled

To Move

Ambled	Moved	Stepped out
Crept	Padded	Stepped off
Danced	Ran	Strode
Departed	Rushed	Strolled
Edged	Sashayed	Stumbled
Hurried	Sauntered	Tip-toed
Hustled	Shambled	Tripped
Left	Slipped	Walked
Lunged	Slogged	Went away
Marched	Sneaked/snuck	
Meandered	Sprinted	

APPENDIX B

How about architectural terms? http://www.aviewoncities.com/_architecturalterms.htm

APPENDIX C

NOTES ON CONFERENCE PLANNING

Why have a conference at all? What is the unifying purpose?

20Booksto50k was a premise that Michael Anderle had. It's based on simple math, breaking down the numbers to yield a bite-sized chunk in order to earn a living wage from your writing.

It's about being a professional author. That means, selling your books. Finding readers willing to buy your books. Our unifying purpose for 20Books Vegas was about indies helping indies. Everyone is in a different spot on their journey.

Everyone needs a different tidbit of information to get them over that next hump. We all need the same information. We all need different information. We need it at different times. And then sometimes, we can forge our own way ahead. But someone else has already done it successfully, while others have failed. Take the good lessons and forge ahead.

Leave the bad lessons by the wayside.

Find a unifying purpose and you'll have a reason to hold a conference.

APPENDIX C

Arrange Guest Speakers simultaneously with reserving space

Talk about chicken and the egg. Until you know your guest speakers and the number of people who may attend, you will have a hard time finding the right-sized space.

For 20Books Vegas, we reserved a room that could handle 650 people, but our break-even point was 250. That gave us a lot of room. How did we know what our break-even point was? That will come later, something else that you need to know before you've even started.

We called places and checked online, but until we had an incredible volunteer go to Vegas and beat on the doors of a dozen hotels and conference centers, we didn't have a place to call our own. Finally, Sam's Town came back to us with the best offer in regards to rooms.

Negotiating points:

- Cost of the conference room can be waived by guaranteeing a certain catering minimum
- Room nights (number of nights that your conference attendees stay in the hotel – the higher the room nights, the more clout you have in negotiating)
- Electronics – most hotels have exclusivity contracts as in, you can't bring your own stuff in. They grossly overcharge, but that's how they pad their bottom line. They'll give you a price list. Understand what you are getting and ask yourself, do you really need it? We encouraged our guest speakers not to have anything that needed to be projected. Cost savings was nearly $1000 by using handouts in packets instead
- Extra outlets in the conference room – this is a pure cost, but in this day and age, being able to plug-in during a long day's conference has a great value, since most conference rooms have almost no outlets. We paid $1500

for 300 extra outlets scattered throughout our conference room
- Breakout rooms – these can be clumped in with your main room. Make sure you have enough space for everything you are trying to accomplish. Give the people room. Being squashed in isn't the best learning environment, either in the main room or breakout rooms
- Wifi for your conference room may be extra – verify that
- Rental for your audio/visual equipment is by the day, not for the full event
- The cost to rent for a half day or a full day could be the same. If it is, just take the room for the full day and that way the hotel will have it set up early so you can put out some banners do other prep-work without issue if you need to because you'll own the space
- Catering – if you have your people there for a full day, get them something to eat. To control your conference schedule, it's better to pay to feed them than to have them disappear. Sure, we're all adults, but the value that you deliver requires a little bit of leading the thoroughbreds to water.
- IT Questions to ask your hotel:
- Is the provided wifi sufficient to live-stream the presentation? If not, how can we get at least one exclusive high-speed internet connection?
- What is the connectivity to the projection system (such as, HDMI male or female)? Will tech support be available? Who is our Point of Contact for issues related to the room during the conference? (And please include a phone number.)
- Will there be outlets for the computer to be used to drive the projector?
- How many microphones will we have available? We need at least two cordless, preferably three, and how can

we ensure they don't run out of juice during the show? (i.e. what battery size do they take)
- Can we hook up audio to the system to play music during the breaks? What connector will we need to accomplish this?

Controlling Attendee Numbers

Gauging the number of guests is important. You have to have a ballpark figure to get started, but dialing in the catering numbers takes real signups. I recommend a cost structure that helps you rein things in.

- From when you open registration until three months prior to the show, charge your first price. In this case, $99.
- From three months to two months, charge your second price ($199).
- At two months out, you should be able to order your swag, badges, and stuff like that. The people who paid the extra registration amount will cover the costs and risks as you hedge forward. Order more than what the numbers show.
- At two months and less to showtime, it is best if you have registration locked, but doing that is hard. You'll have people fall out and others who could use what you're pushing at your convention. From two months to one month, I recommend something on the order of $299 to offset any costs associated with last-minute phone calls to the venue to up your numbers.

Using price to encourage earlier signup and discourage late signups is one way to help you control your numbers, or at least cover the costs associated with last-minute additions.

The Schedule

Keep in mind your general conference theme. Begin with the end in mind. At the end of the conference, how do you want people to feel?

Build them up one piece at a time as if you are building a house. Start with the foundation. Set the expectations of a shared journey and make sure everyone knows what is going on. Having both a printed and digitally available schedule is important. Conference attendees will get frustrated if they don't know where they need to be and when they need to be there.

The Space

More chicken and egg stuff. If you plan to do things that require people to write or type on their laptops, then give them the space to do that. Tables are best for ergonomics, but don't have the attendees sitting on top of each other. If the conference room says it can seat 250, DO NOT put 250 people in there. They won't have room to move.

In Vegas, we rented a space that could hold 650 people and we capped the conference at 400. We'll have tables and plenty of space to move around. We'll have snacks and drinks available throughout. (Budget for this and make sure you know the full costs. In Vegas, whatever the catering cost shows, we need to add 26.25% because of taxes and mandatory gratuity.)

The Guest Speakers

These good people are your drawing power. You need to give them the red carpet treatment. For 20Books Vegas, we were truly blessed by having an all-star cast volunteer to speak with us, and they even paid their own way. What an incredible testament to our premise of indies giving back to indies.

Of course, it doesn't hurt to have the venue in a place that doubles as a neat vacation spot. Another point to consider when organizing a conference. Make sure you are able to share the other amenities offered at your location. You can post links online or share information in the handout packet.

Pre-Conference Prep

Stay in touch with the hotel. If you aren't on a first-name basis with everyone who has anything to do with your show, you're doing it wrong. Don't be a pest, but be complimentary and make sure you haven't assumed anything. Keeping everything in writing will help you have a shared understanding of your conference.

The hotel is there to make sure you have a good experience. Some things you want may have an additional cost. Understanding that up front and what those costs will be will go a long ways in making sure that you don't add stress and friction to your lives.

A step-by-step walk-through of what you want as you are shaping your conference helps immensely. If you can't do the in-person thing, then you will need to spend some time on the phone.

Have both digital and printed copies of the material you want each attendee to have. We bought a high-capacity printer solely for this purpose as we were going to have about 5000 pages of printed matter to hand out. We cleaned out Walmart for their folders, but it was the best price and one-stop shopping.

You'll need to start printing stuff early, but don't start too early because things will change! You only want to print and stuff folders one time. We had an incredible volunteer to do all that for us and arrived at the show in a minivan packed with ready-to-go folders.

Make sure that you are aligned with your electronics package. Just know that you'll have to pay the price for the projector, screen, and sound system. Get it right and ensure that your guest speakers are able to project whatever they want. We asked them to bring their own computers so we didn't have to deal with software compatibility issues. We knew the projector had an HDMI interface. We informed the guest speakers, and we had a volunteer who coordinated it all, to include bringing extra interface cables just in case.

Signing Up and Paying

This will present your first technical challenge. We created a unique website, and built in WordPress with embedded forms with PayPal.

It took a few trials and errors to get this right before we went live, but we had no problems with it at all. We paid for both WP plugins to make sure that we had technical support to resolve any issues.

Here is the information we collected for the signup:

- Real Name (mandatory field)
- Pen Name
- Name for your badge (mandatory field and to share publicly as part of the published attendee roster)
- Address
- Email Address (mandatory field)
- Website (to share publicly)
- Primary genre you write in
- Secondary genre
- Number of published novels (this is not a mandatory field, but I threw folks for a loop by not having an option for "0". Next time, I'll make sure that 0 is one of the drop downs. 0, 1, 2-3, 4-5, 6-10, 11-15, and 16+.
- Number of published works other than novels (drop down with 0, 1, 2-3, 4-5, 6-10, 11-15, and 16+).
- PayPal email address (mandatory field – used for verification of payment only)
- Cups of coffee that you'll drink each day (this was to best guesstimate the catering numbers – non-mandatory field)
- Cups of tea (again, catering)

APPENDIX C

- Number of donuts you'll eat (again, catering)
- Biography (a free-form paragraph for information that the attendee is willing to share publicly)
- General annual revenue (not mandatory, but won't be made public – we used this for a general show demographic) Dropdown boxes for 0-$10k, $10k-$50k, $50k-$100k, >$100k)
- Will you be staying at the venue (mandatory field) (This was to bounce off the hotel to see if we were meeting our obligation. We received a nice cost break because for a conference with an estimated 300 attendees, we gave them over 1000 room nights.)

A total of five mandatory fields was all for our tracking purposes. The integrated PayPal app worked superbly, although some people were able to sign up (about 2%) and record their data without finishing through PayPal. We simply sent them an invoice and half paid. The others bailed out, but at least we knew.

I issued refunds for the show right up until I submitted the final catering numbers. If I received a request for a refund, I jumped on PayPal right there and sent it to them. I didn't want anyone to think we were anything less that forthright with the show's funds.

Swag

Make sure you have some graphics skills or have a volunteer with the skills as each of the below services wants their graphics in a little bit different format and at different resolutions.

- Badges – 4imprint.com
- Lanyards – nationallanyard.net
- Pens & Notebooks – pens.com
- Cups, t-shirts, towels, notebook covers, & more – society6.com

Volunteers

You need help. A great deal of help. People are willing to help, but don't abuse that trust. Know what you need to do, set clear expectations, and be patient. The conference director does about 90% of the work, but that last 10% is critical to show success. The volunteers will take care of that and they will be the face of the show.

You can't be in all places at all times. Break out the tasks and get help. Here's what we did for 20Books Vegas.

- Breakout room coordinators – responsible for schedule (in case of ad hoc sessions), posting the name placards of the speakers in those rooms, and generally keeping things on track in the smaller rooms
- Attendee packet printing & stuffing
- Raffle coordinator – run the raffles at the show
- Guest speaker IT coordinator – make sure of no technical glitches
- Check-in desk coordinator
- General assistant to the director (I need help at the show because I want to help everyone)
- Logistics coordinator – someone who lived locally and had space. We incrementally shipped our swag and other conference stuff to him and then he delivered it on the morning of the show where we had plenty of hands to help.

Advertisers

The conference represents an organization or a brand or something unique that has drawn your attendees. We initially contemplated sponsors, but then canceled that idea because we didn't want to be in a position to vet those who would donate to the show. We didn't want to promote one service over another.

APPENDIX C

We dispensed with sponsors and went with advertisers and supporters. We set up an advertisement with half or full-page full-color print ads with a corresponding piece on the web page. Simple as that. We posted a disclaimer that the conference was not responsible for claims or services made by individual advertisers.

We also added a conference donation button. By running lean and not profiting from the show, we limited catering. Donations helped us keep some of the nice things to have like doughnuts, fruit, and cookies for all the sessions.

Conference Check In

Keeping this easy is critical! People should only need their name. If they aren't on the list, your check-in crew should have a laptop and a way to check/verify that the person paid. With authors, so many have multiple names, they may not exactly know under which name they signed up. If you have a list of real names, then you must control that!

Many authors do not want their real name associated with their pen name. Respect their privacy by controlling access to their information. Have this as a backup along with PayPal receipt info. I expect you won't have issues, since this isn't something that generally comes up.

We had very nice badges printed (or a sponsor could provide) with a blank space for attendees to write whatever they wanted for their name. If you pre-print them, they look nicer, but what a logistics nightmare for check-in and re-printing. People change their minds on what they want to share. Tell them that they'll write their own name. Have sharpies at the check-in table.

Swag should be pre-packed. One set for each paid attendee. We went with a pen and notebook, because we do writers' conferences. We imprinted the logo on the notebook and did a nice print and our tagline on the pen, which had a metallic barrel with the rubber-tip that could be used to tap on a touchscreen. They were about triple the cost of the cheapest pens, but cheap pens are exactly that. Show some class.

Dress for the job you want, right?

Health Concerns

Make sure that you know your audience. All conference facilities should accommodate those with disabilities. But what about allergies and things like that?

We bought the Purell wipes and included a couple in each attendee's packet. We also put bottles of hand sanitizer on the tables —not all, but a good sampling—in addition to boxes of facial tissues.

Make the people comfortable and they'll have a better conference. Don't just take their money and put on a program. Show them that you care.

Keeping to your schedule

Someone has to ride herd on the guest speakers. Some will talk for as long as you let them, while some will run short, but it doesn't even out. The chances of running long are far greater than getting done early. The conference director has the ominous task of keeping the schedule on track.

I put in long breaks to help us flex and generally only two forty-five minute sessions back to back. That makes it easier on the crowd as you don't want people trapped in their seats for more than an hour and a half at a pop. They need to get up and reenergize.

And the 20Books conference is about networking as much as the presentations. How can you do that if there's no time to stand around, drink coffee, and talk?

Be ready to flex. This is the value of an online schedule. If a guest speaker can't make it at the last minute, that's okay. That happens. Your guest speakers are important people with families. Have a backup in mind and ready to go. I had a presentation ready should a fill-in be required, since I was going to be in the main room at all times anyway.

The Raffles

We had a raffle at the beginning of each section following a break. We bought a bunch of 20Books gear (notebook holders, insulated mugs, etc) and we took donations of non-fiction books relating to self-publishing.

Each badge had a number and we had the raffle tickets for those numbers. This way, no one lost their ticket and it encouraged people to get back on time because of the cool packages that were raffled away. Must be present to win.

We wanted to keep the 20Books brand (a concept, not a commercial product) front and center during the show, so we added a raffle for anyone sporting the 20Books gear, which we had made well before the show. When we spotted someone wearing the gear, we gave them a raffle ticket, putting the other half in a bucket to be drawn each day. We had three different editing packages donated, and these were the 20Books gear raffle prizes. We selected a ticket at the end of each day. (Must be present to win!)

General Timeline

One year to eighteen months before the show

- Determine conference purpose and general number of attendees
- Find venue location and sign contract
- Send out feelers for guest speakers

Six to nine months out

- Build website

APPENDIX C

- Start taking signups
- Build newsletter list
- Rough out schedule
- Advertise and get people to sign up so you can solidify your numbers

Three to six months out

- Send newsletters and share information
- Order your gear (we had over 400 signups so we ordered 500 of everything with the intent to sell the excess pens and notebooks at the show)

One to three months out

- Don't panic, but the pace picks up at this point
- Confirm with the hotel any details that you can't confirm (check and recheck your paperwork)
- Keep the attendees informed – start building excitement with a countdown to the show
- Stay in touch with the guest speakers (one thing we did for the show was buy really nice gifts for the guest speakers since they paid their own way—we bought these out of our pockets, because we wanted everyone to feel that they were getting the red carpet treatment)
- First rough draft of conference table setup
- First draft of electronics package for the show
- Rally the volunteers—they will save you from getting gray hairs
- Understand the status of everything you have ordered (if you wait until one month before the show to order, you will cause yourself undue stress and risk not getting something in time)

APPENDIX C

One to four weeks before the show

- This is the home stretch where you keep thinking that you've forgotten something
- Stay in touch with your volunteers, keep them motivated without overtasking them
- Stay in touch with your guest speakers—make sure you have the materials they need to share with the attendees (both digitally posted on the website as well as in printable form)
- Verify everything that will go into the packets and set it up. Print the attendee materials and stuff the folders
- Prepare the badges as much as you need to (for us, it was labeling each one with a number for the raffles)
- Confirm final catering numbers with the venue
- Confirm final electronics package with the venue
- Confirm conference room setup with the venue
- Keep the excitement going with the attendees—maybe send an NL a week with a countdown
- Firm up schedule details and share with the attendees (as well as wait to the last minute to print this one, just in case)

One week up to C-Day

- The director needs to show up early, meet with the venue, show them some love, maybe bring gifts (I'm from Alaska so brought some Alaskana for my POCs that had been so helpful in the buildup to the show)
- Meet with volunteers they day before or the morning that you need them in order to shake hands—they need to be comfortable with you and you with them
- Delineate tasks and do a walkabout. All need to know the

venue so they don't get lost and can answer questions from late arrivals
- Verify that the conference room setup meets your needs as early as possible, so there's time to fix things
- Time is your greatest friend—validate all conference elements as early as possible. Our room was supposed to be set up the night before, so that's when I checked on it, just to be sure.
- Show up early and dress for success. You are the person that everyone will know. Be confident, know your details, and answer questions patiently if you can't turn someone over to a volunteer (my general assistant because he saved me from getting quagmired in long conversations when stuff needed to be done)
- Check-in desk must run smoothly—one person in charge of the sheet to check off people as they check-in, and then to give out the badges, lanyards, packages, and swag. Control these or you'll run out before everyone checks in.
- Verify catering and any provided meals
- Put contact numbers into your speed dial so you can call and resolve issues like room temperature or electronics failure during the show
- Ensure the electronics work (IT volunteer) and that you have all cables, connectors, and dongles, as well as chargers or extra batteries for the cordless microphones
- Give a great welcome aboard speech

INDEX

20Booksto50K, 15, 21, 29, 63, 100, 119, 130-132, 142, 146, 150, 153-154

Aaron, Rachel, 137
ACX (audiobooks), 25, 31, 139
Adobe, 49
aggregators, 66
AKreport, 22
Alaska, 4, 14, 20, 31, 35, 156, 160, 163
Amazon Affiliate program, 25
Amazon KDP, 22, 24, 28, 31-33, 35-38, 49, 56, 59-60, 65-66, 90, 103, 136, 139
AMS ads (Amazon Marketing Services), 7, 22-23, 32, 56, 65, 67-68, 73, 79, 89, 108-109, 139
Anderle, Michael, 4-5, 14, 33, 116, 142, 158-159
anthologies, 6, 75-76, 87, 89, 160-162
AOL, 73
Apple iBooks, 48, 106
audiobooks, 25-26, 90, 139, 158-160

INDEX

Author Central (Amazon), 37, 50, 61
author rank, 3, 26-28, 99, 113-115

backlist, 3, 11-12, 29, 33, 86, 89-90, 106-107
Bad Company (series), 23-24, 26, 28, 115, 159
Baldwin, James Osiris, 9, 138
Bali, 28, 119, 130
BargainBooksy, 16, 105
Barnes & Noble, 48, 107
bestsellers, 3, 59-60, 65, 96, 113, 118, 130
Blasty, 43
Blurb, 66
blurbs, 2, 7, 15, 32, 36-37, 46, 49, 56-59, 64, 94, 98-99
Book Barbarian, 64
BookBub, 3, 11, 13, 15, 26, 79, 102, 110-111, 139
BookFunnel, 10, 15, 49, 75-76,
BookReport, 22-23, 24-25, 32-33, 90

Carr, Martha, 161
Chesson, Dave, 60, 136
Christmas, 55, 124
CMI (Craig Martelle, Inc), 31
Cohen, Bryan, 57, 136
collaborations, 3, 25-26, 33, 41, 88, 90, 113, 116-118
conference planning, 142-157
conventions, 1, 3, 14-16, 113, 119-120, 145
Cook, Glen, 16
Cooper, Michael, 79, 105, 109, 126, 135
Cooper, Sheldon (character on Big Bang Theory), 98
copyrights, 2, 9, 20, 34, 42-44
Corder, Honoree, 135
cover art, 2-3, 23, 28, 37, 46, 49, 52-53, 55, 68, 72-74, 76, 87, 89, 93, 95, 99, 145
Coyne, Shawn, 137

INDEX

CPC (cost-per-click), 109
Createspace, 16, 25, 31, 66
Cynus Space Opera, 4, 58-59, 160

Darklanding (series), 17, 21, 47, 56-57, 65, 69, 160
Dawson, Mark, 8, 136
DepositPhoto, 74
derivative rights, 117
Dickens, Charles, A Tale of Two Cities, 13
digital rights management, 2, 46
Disney, 35
Draft2Digital (D2D), 28, 36, 48, 66
Drake, Maxwell Alexander, 19, 137

Earle, Michael-Scott, 161
Edinburgh, 119
EIN (employer identification number), 29, 31, 38
email list, 1, 6, 75-79, 158
Ereader News Today (ENT), 64, 94, 105, 139
Expanding Universe, The, 161

Facebook, 2-3, 7-8, 10, 13-15, 18, 21, 23, 30, 32, 51, 63, 73-74, 76, 78-79, 83, 99, 102-103, 109, 111, 135, 158
Faulks, Kim, 164
Firefly, 47-48, 68-69, 160
Fox, Chris, 135, 161
Fox, Richard, 56-57
FreeBooksy, 15
Free Trader (series), 4, 30, 32, 55, 58, 65, 73, 94, 106, 159-160

GaryCon X, 161
Gaughran, David, 110, 134
giveaways, 3, 6-7, 12, 42, 63, 78
goals, 3, 17, 33, 86-87, 96, 125

INDEX

Goodreads, 50-51
Google, 4, 16, 30-31, 35, 43, 66, 117
Grahl, Tim, 137

Haldeman, Joe, 16
Hale, Ben, 135
Harry Potter books, 1, 26, 102
Howey, Hugh, 8, 96
Hollywood, 130

ICON (Cedar Rapids), 14
IngramSpark, 31, 66
InstaFreebie, 10, 75
Instagram, 13, 30, 73
IRS (Internal Revenue Service), 29, 31, 38-41, 163

James, E.L., 81
Jutoh, 49

KDP (Amazon's Kindle Direct Publishing), 22, 24, 28, 31-33, 35-38, 49, 56, 59-60, 65-66, 90, 103, 136, 139
KDP Rocket, 35, 56, 60, 136
KENP, 33, 139
keywords, 2, 46-47, 49, 56-57, 61, 98
Kobo, 16, 28, 48, 66
King, Stephen, 26

lawyers, 19, 34, 37, 40, 98, 118, 163
LLC (limited liability company), 31, 37-39
LMBPN Publishing, 5
Lord of the Rings, The, 32
Lulu, 66

MailChimp, 7, 10

INDEX

mailing list, 1, 6, 75-79, 158
Marine Corps, 21, 90, 116
McLaughlin, Kevin, 6-8, 161
McCaffrey, Anne, 32
Meeks, Brian, 22, 58, 79, 109, 126, 134
Microsoft Word, 16
military science fiction, 6, 24, 30, 110, 115
Minimal Viable Product (MVP), 13-15, 23, 117, 132
Moon, Scott, 47, 68, 160

Nassise, Joe, 19
Nebula Award, 89, 119, 161
newsletters, 1, 2, 7-11, 13-15, 50, 55, 61, 64, 65, 71, 75-76, 78-79, 88, 99, 102, 106-107, 125, 139, 154, 158
non-fiction, 35, 153, 158

Oxford comma, 132-133

Patterson, James, 96, 124
PayPal, 41, 148-149, 152
pen names, 1, 17, 83, 117, 148, 151
Permuted Press, 36, 160
post-apocalyptic, 2, 116
POV (points of view), 31, 89

raffles, 150, 153-155
Reacher, Jack (Lee Child character), 26
ReadCheaply, 15
Readerlinks, 22
revenue, 1, 20-22, 29, 31, 33, 38-39, 90, 97, 103-105, 149
Robin Reads, 64, 94, 105
romance, 19, 80, 119
Rowling, JK, 1, 10-11, 26, 102, 128,

INDEX

Scrivener, 16, 49
serials, 2, 46, 48, 56, 68, 87
SFWA (Science Fiction and Fantasy Writers of America), 119, 127
Smashwords, 66
social proof, 3, 86, 94-95
Solari, Joe, 37-38, 138, 163
space opera, 4, 6, 24, 30, 48, 56, 58, 60, 68, 75-77, 87, 160
starter library (Martelle), 10, 161
Story Grid, The, 137
Story Shop, 31
StreetLib, 66
Syme, Chris, 136
synonyms, 3, 18, 140-141
SWOT analysis, 20, 35-36

taxes, 2, 20-21, 38-42, 99, 146
thrillers, 160-161
Tolkien, JRR, 31-32
Trackerbox, 22
trolls, 2, 17, 71, 82-83
Twitter, 7, 13, 30, 73, 158

USS Gerald R. Ford (aircraft carrier), 90

Walmart, 108, 147
Walton, Terry Henry, 4, 13, 24, 30, 64, 116, 158-159
Ward, James M., 161-162
whale readers, 12

YouTube, 29, 98

POSTSCRIPT

If you liked this book, please give it a little love and leave a review. I'm not big on non-fiction. My wheelhouse is Science Fiction! So, you don't need to join my newsletter as I'm not going to promote non-fiction there. But if you like Science Fiction...

You can join my mailing list by dropping by my website www.craigmartelle.com or if you have any comments, shoot me a note at craig@craigmartelle.com. I am always happy to hear from people who've read my work. I try to answer every email I receive.

You can also follow me on the various social media pages that I frequent.

Amazon – www.amazon.com/author/craigmartelle
Facebook – www.faceBook.com/authorcraigmartelle
My web page – www.craigmartelle.com
Twitter – www.twitter.com/rick_banik

OTHER BOOKS BY CRAIG MARTELLE

The Terry Henry Walton Chronicles, a Kurtherian Gambit Series, co-written with Michael Anderle

- World's Worst Day Ever (a short prequel of sorts)
- Book 1 – Nomad Found (also available on audiobook)
- Book 2 – Nomad Redeemed (also available on audiobook)
- Book 3 - Nomad Unleashed (also available on audiobook)
- Book 4 - Nomad Supreme (also available on audiobook)
- Book 5 – Nomad's Fury (also available on audiobook)
- Book 6 – Nomad's Justice (also available on audiobook)
- Book 7 – Nomad Avenged (also available on audiobook)
- Book 8 – Nomad Mortis (also available on audiobook)
- Book 9 – Nomad's Force (also available on audiobook)
- Book 10 – Nomad's Galaxy (also available on audiobook)
- Nomad's Journal – A collection of Terry Henry Walton Short Stories

The Bad Company – with Michael Anderle

- Book 0 – Gateway to the Universe (with Justin Sloan)
- Book 1 – The Bad Company
- Book 2 – Blockade
- Book 3 – Price of Freedom
- Book 4 – Liberation
- And more coming

Superdreadnought – with Michael Anderle

- Book 1 – Alone & Unafraid

- Book 2 – something else

The Kurtherian Barrister

- Book 1

Free Trader Series

- Book 1 – The Free Trader of Warren Deep
- Book 2 – The Free Trader of Planet Vii
- Book 3 – Adventures on RV Traveler
- Book 4 – Battle for the Amazon
- Book 5 – Free the North!
- Book 6 – Free Trader on the High Seas
- Book 7 – Southern Discontent
- Book 8 – The Great 'Cat Rebellion (2018)
- Book 9 – Return to the Traveler (2018)
- Outpost of the Ancients – a Free Trader short story published in the Apocalyptic Space Collection, Volume 1

Cygnus Space Opera – set in the Free Trader Universe

- Book 1 – Cygnus Rising
- Book 2 – Cygnus Expanding
- Book 3 – Cygnus Arrives
- Cygnus Omnibus – Books 1 to 3 under one cover and also as an audiobook

Darklanding – a serial space western (Firefly meets Tombstone) co-written with Scott Moon

- Book 1 – Assignment: Darklanding
- Book 2 – Ike Shot the Sheriff

- Book 3 – Outlaws
- Darklanding Omni 1 (contains books 1-3, also on audio)
- Book 4 – Runaway
- Book 5 – An Unglok Murder
- Book 6 – SAGCON (coming Mar 16)
- Book 7 – Race to the Finish (coming Apr 2)
- Book 8 – Boomtown (coming April Apr 20)
- Book 9 – A Warrior's Home (coming May 8)
- Book 10 – TBD
- Book 11 – TBD
- Book 12 – TBD

End Times Alaska Series, a Permuted Press publication

- Book 1: Endure (also available on audiobook)
- Book 2: Run (also available on audiobook)
- Book 3: Return (also available on audiobook)
- Book 4: Fury (also available on audiobook)

Rick Banik Thrillers

- People Raged and the Sky Was on Fire (also available on audiobook)
- The Heart Raged (coming)
- Paranoid in Paradise – a short story within the Close to Bones Anthology

The Human Experiment – a novel, co-written with Kevin McLaughlin

Short Stories (and where you can find them)

- The Misadventures of Jacob Wild McKilljoy (with Michael-Scott Earle) (Always FREE)
- Just One More Fight (published as a novella standalone)

- Wisdom's Journey (published as a novella standalone)
- Fear Peace (published as a short story standalone)
- Paranoid in Paradise (a Rick Banik Thriller in the Close to the Bones Anthology)
- The Trenches of Centauri Prime
- The Outcast (Through the Never Anthology, nominated for consideration for a Nebula Award)
- Defense of the Deep Space Denali (in The Expanding Universe Vol 2)
- A Language Barrier (in The Expanding Universe Vol 3, also nominated for Nebula consideration)
- Mystically Engineered (in Tales from the Void, a Chris Fox Anthology)
- Cruiseliner Hades 7, a Lost 77 Worlds Tale (written at GaryCon X)

Box Sets & Anthologies

- Trader, Cygnus, & People Raged – Martelle Starter Library
- Close to the Bones, a Thriller Anthology (edited by Martha Carr)
- The Expanding Universe, Volume 1 (edited by Craig Martelle)
- The Expanding Universe, Volume 2 (edited by Craig Martelle)
- The Expanding Universe, Volume 3 (edited by Craig Martelle)
- Earth Prime Anthology, Volume 1 (Stephen Lee & James M. Ward)
- Apocalyptic Space Short Story Collection (Stephen Lee & James M. Ward)
- Lunar Resorts Anthology, Volume 2 (Stephen Lee & James M. Ward)

- Rise of Juneau, a Blasted Earth Game Module (Stephen Lee & James M. Ward)
- Metamorphosis Alpha – Chronicles from the Warden Vol 1 (with James M. Ward, edited by Craig Martelle)
- Metamorphosis Alpha – Chronicles from the Warden Vol 2 (with James M. Ward, edited by Craig Martelle)

AUTHOR NOTES

I am the blue collar author. I have a law degree, but that doesn't matter, not when it comes to writing. What matters is the willingness to work hard at this thing called self-publishing. I've worked harder, not smarter, on a number of things. I've been fairly successful, but I have so much more to learn.

Part of what helps me to learn is trying to help others. That's what this book is all about. I am sharing what I've done, and I've made many mistakes, some more costly than others. I want to help you avoid those mistakes while also telling you that you aren't alone.

Shout out to my friend, Joe Solari, who provided some good input regarding the business section. Check out his business books. He knows what he's talking about.

Some of the other authors I reference are friends and that is the strangest of things. Three years ago, I was freezing my ass off on the North Slope of Alaska working as a business consultant. Now, I have friends who are household names in the huge industry of self-publishing. I know people who are at the tops of their genre lists. And sometimes, the book up there is the one I wrote. It's crazy how things can happen when you realize what you were meant to do.

But I wouldn't be me without all of the stuff in between. I don't think I could write compelling combat scenes without having been in war. I couldn't have written how that affects people without having witnessed it firsthand. It's all fun and games until you get issued grenades.

And the lawyer in me says that I should help people who are less inclined to enjoy reading statements from the IRS or your state's department of trade and business.

So, here I am, trying to share what I've learned. Although writing is a lonely profession, you don't have to be alone, just like I wasn't in writing this book.

Shout out to Kim Faulks, who helped me with the writing motivation section. Being creative is a very personal endeavor—it's not like getting in your car and driving to work. When you sit down at your computer and look at a blank screen, that can be daunting. But it starts with the first word, the first stick figure, then you add flesh, background, and color. You add other characters and you're off and running. Thanks, Kim, for helping me make that section a little more robust.

Shout out to the review crew! What a great bunch of people.

- Andy McWain
- Drew A. Avera
- Ellie Keating
- Ira Heinichen
- J. Clifton Slater
- John R. Monteith
- Kelly Bowerman
- Scott Sakatch

Thank you all. You helped make this book better and more helpful through your valuable input.

Made in the USA
Columbia, SC
11 April 2023